SUPER MARKETWALA

SECRETS TO WINNING CONSUMER INDIA

DAMODAR MALL

PORTFOLIO
PENGUIN

An imprint of Penguin Random House

PORTFOLIO

USA | Canada | UK | Ireland | Australia
New Zealand | India | South Africa | China | Singapore

Portfolio is part of the Penguin Random House group of companies whose addresses can be found at global.penguinrandomhouse.com

Published by Penguin Random House India Pvt. Ltd
4th Floor, Capital Tower 1, MG Road,
Gurugram 122 002, Haryana, India

Penguin Random House India

First published by Random House India 2014
This edition published by Penguin Random House India 2020

10 9 8 7 6 5 4 3

ISBN 9788184003857

Typeset in Electra LT by R. Ajith Kumar
Printed at Repro India Limited

www.penguin.co.in

FSC www.fsc.org MIX Paper from responsible sources FSC® C047271

This is a legitimate digitally printed version of the book and therefore might not have certain extra finishing on the cover.

To the woman home manager.
She pays my wages and shapes my business.
This book is a tribute to her.

Contents

Foreword

INDIA HAS BEEN A cradle of civilization since time immemorial. As one of the earliest major civilizations in the world, Indians have always had an original point of view about life, philosophy, worldly matters, and political strategy, as well as a preferred way of life. India's influence was carried far and wide around the world through trade relationships and spiritual thought leaders. However, this influence started to dissipate as India witnessed armed conquests and colonization. When a country is poor and enslaved, as India was for a very long time, the ability to assert its thoughts and preferences becomes dormant in the face of day-to-day struggles of survival. As a result, it was a long time before marketers acknowledged and serviced these preferences.

Contemporary India, however, is a far cry from the India of ten or even five years ago. Today, as more and more of us prosper and aspire to a better life, our collective preferences are growing and flourishing like never before. Not only are we now being served by global markets, we are also shaping them in turn.

The modern Indian is a confident consumer who knows what she wants—her preferences and habits are every bit as international as the next global citizen. However, modern Indian consumers have a unique personality—they have not given up on all things Indian. They proudly retain their 'Indianness'—including their culture and traditions, rites and rituals, and art—and their preferences and habits reflect this ethos. For this reason, the reality of the Indian market is tough for marketers— being experienced doesn't necessarily translate into being right, and being new doesn't have to mean being wrong. Retail, along with many other sectors in India, is undergoing a series of transformations and retailers must adopt a new line of thinking and utilise new interpreters to help navigate the uncharted waters of this dynamic new marketplace.

And what exactly makes this new market dynamic? In most of Europe and North America, retail modernisation took place after their markets were already middle income, consuming markets. The advent of modern retail brought further efficiency, scale and value to their markets. However, the journey of modern retail in India will take a different path. India has a large and culturally inclined population that is just evolving into the middle-class. This middle-class will need a modern retail model that will not merely serve consumption efficiently, but redefine consumption itself. In fact, the Indian telecom sector witnessed growth on similar lines. Mobile phones became accessible to a very large number of Indian consumers even before wired landline phones became ubiquitous. As a result, the telecom sector jumped a stage in its evolution. Similarly, it will not take India decades to build distribution networks across the country.

India's complex marketplace has challenged many a wise

man. Many large players have realized that it is not only about setting up a large store with a wide variety of goods and waiting for the consumer to walk in. Damodar Mall, one of the leading experts on India's retail sector, busts this myth among many others in *Supermarketwala*. Damodar highlights ways in which Indian retail is different—and how marketers can use this difference to their advantage, as well as to the benefit of the customer. *Supermarketwala* provides deep insight into the psyche of the Indian consumer, answering questions like: What should a store layout be like? What do wide aisles indicate, as opposed to crowded ones? What does ready-to-eat mean in India?

Supermarketwala is both timely and appropriate. Young Indian consumers are aspirational and celebrate choice. Modern marketplaces are no longer only about providing access to great products and experiences; they also fire the imagination of consumers. It's the small things in life that bring joy to us and our families. This book will allow you a glimpse into how you can make these 'small things' that much more special for consumers.

Mukesh Ambani

PREFACE

ALL OF US BELIEVE in the maxim of 'the customer is always right'. But every once in a while we are surprised by the failures we encounter in building our relationships with customers. Is therefore the maxim wrong? Not at all. The common pitfall in almost all such cases is our inability to identify the customer correctly. Most of us in organized, large businesses come from the white collared, upper middle-class, 'credit card' India. We like to work, interact and socialize amongst people like us and therefore, often see the world from only our own lens. Fortunately or unfortunately, we form a very small minority.

In a country of 1.27 billion people, the sheer diversity and factors that drive consumer behaviour are so vast and constantly evolving that it is quite common to miss out on the needs, aspirations and behaviour of our own customers. Professional backgrounds, whether a family is a native or an immigrant in the city, the size and structure of the family unit, and of course language, place of origin, castes, and religious backgrounds—each of these factors play a vital role in shaping customer behaviour. More importantly, in an India that is rapidly evolving and responding to various intrinsic and extrinsic trends and developments, there are various consumer groups that are evolving, moulding, forming and dissolving. For example, by the end of this decade, almost one in every ten Indians will be above the age of 60 years, or that the number of working women has doubled in the past decade, or that almost two-thirds of urban Indians are self-employed.

In India, for almost all categories of consumption, including fashion and apparels, it is not seasons but marriages and festivals that continue to be the prime drivers for consumption in India. And the periods of marriages and festivals differ from community to community, following the lunar, solar, or luni-solar calendars that each of the different communities follow. Each of these factors today shape the way Indians shop tomorrow.

As retail modernizes and new brands and products emerge in the food, home care and personal care segments, brand and retail teams must discuss and design products and services for the real Indian customer, even as she modernises. For that, business teams need a narrative to get a fuller grip on the middle India. For instance, we now have enough years of experience in the retail industry in India to articulate our own unique ways of selling things to Indians. This narrative is worth having, to form a strong foundation for future strategies. While the theory of retail is developing in the corridors of academia, we also need to create an archive of good business practices that connect directly to our social reality. In our development of the retail industry in India, all of us have made our own mistakes, learned from these and these have also helped shape some spectacular triumphs. What were the assumptions underlying all of these? What are the counters to the strategies that we devise from time to time? Can retail exist independent of society? How do social trends impact the way we think 'business'? In the three-legged stool called modern retail, with its foundations of customers, supply partners and store colleagues, what are the dynamics connecting these legs? These and many more questions arise when we discuss business.

Who knows what goes on in the mind of the customer? Does she embrace chaos and sidestep sophistication? Why does she prefer to shop with her family rather than alone? How does she pick and choose from the hundreds of offers that every single marketer seems bent on sending her way? The fact is there is still not enough body of knowledge to create homegrown experts. Everyone is learning along the way, and adding their expertise to the way the story of retail builds in this country. Damodar Mall is amongst a very small number of such experts.

Damodar, in all my interactions with him, has always had the knack of providing just the right articulation. His insights start with sharp customer observation and a mindset that says the customer is right. He knows who his customer is. Equally importantly, he has learnt what makes her happy. This sounds simple enough. And yet, many practitioners of retail find it an extremely complex and bewildering business. If Maggi Noodles is such a runaway hit, why should Ching's Secret have such a different positioning, and yet be so successful? Does India's exotic food future lie in thin crust pizza or pesarattu dosa? Should stores have less 'noise', i.e., promotions, or more? Why do women prefer to travel to a store five kilometres away rather than shop at their neighbourhood kirana?

This book promotes a certain kind of mindset, one that

reposes faith in an India that is becoming increasingly confident. The fact that there are scores of stores that are succeeding with this kind of customer at their core, shows that business managers would do well to follow the precepts laid out by Damodar in *Supermarketwala*. The word *Supermarketwala* itself is percipient. It denotes modernity with a strong connect with the unique culture of India and has all the makings of a brand in itself. No other term could better define what a retailer should think when he thinks 'business in India'.

Supermarketwala takes a critical look at accepted wisdom in retail, and goes on to hypothesise why such theories will succeed or fail in India. We often make the mistake of accepting the word of 'experts' at face value. If a global retail guru talks about the 'butt-and-brush' factor, it is but natural for us to work on that. We forget that he is speaking to a market that has evolved differently from India, and is culturally the equivalent of the North Pole for us. *Supermarketwala* gives us the 'Elbow Push' factor instead, and we suddenly realise how much more appropriate it is to our unique circumstances of constant strife in public spaces.

Modern retail has been reviled by many public figures as a dehumanising concept. Is that really true in India, where social inequity is a daily reality for the vast majority? How many of us have bothered to look at its liberating aspects, and how it lends itself to greater democracy? 'Temples of Democracy' gives us an altogether different insight into what modern retail spaces are beginning to stand for in our country.

The cross learning between global and local of the kind, 'Thank You McDonald, Welcome Idli Factory' piece in the book narrates, is the sweet spot for consumer business success in India, in my view.

There were times when only cold drinks and leftovers were kept in the refrigerators in India. There may be times when people will stack them up fully with frozen foods or cook over weekends and freeze their dinners for eating on week-days. Between these two milestones of consumption behaviour is a long journey.

India is the only market where even in upmarket homes, every old newspaper and every plastic pack of milk is given out for recycling. This book calls it our 'social technology' of shared good habits that will help consuming India be more frugal and green, compared to the western societies.

I am especially happy that Damodar has chosen to bring in the impact of modern retail on its store associates and small vendors as well. These 'constituencies' of retail must be celebrated much more. His chapter on 'Unexpected Ripples of Goodness', left a special impression on me since it deals with the positivity a young woman associates with the profession of retail that she takes back to her entire family.

Two other thought leaders, B.S. Nagesh and Santosh Desai, have been allies who helped shape my point of view on the modernising Indian market. I'm glad some facets of their thinking is also showcased in *Supermarketwala.* And then there are the unique stories of how wholly homegrown brands have emerged almost out of nowhere and proceeded to take the Indian market by storm. I'm proud of the contribution modern retail has made to their success, and very happy to see some of these stories shared here.

Modern retail is shaping as a clear flag bearer of aspiring India. This is where our new sense of well-being finds expression and it is on this theatre of choice that the good things in life become accessible to mainstream India. It has always been my belief that modernising retail has to be just a couple of steps ahead of the customer, not more, if its benefits have to reach larger numbers. Our social fabric is quite strong and resilient—we tend to blend change and tradition in a continuous flow. For the new brands and stores that are symbols of modernity, the biggest prize lies just a step ahead of the customers.

Kishore Biyani

Sao Paulo to Raigad Bazaar

'WHY ARE SO MANY men standing in a half-hour queue on a Sunday afternoon, to buy toothpaste and biscuits, under an asbestos roof?'

That incisive question to me, from ace stock market punter R.K. Damani and our joint search for its answer at Raigad Bazaar, Alibaug, 90 kms from Mumbai was going to change completely the course of my life, and eventually his, too. We were at this simple, basic supermarket run by a 'farmers and workers co-operative' in small-town Alibaug, on our curiosity trip of supermarkets, in 1999. Back then, supermarkets were few and far between in India and the few in Mumbai region, Apna Bazaar, Sahakari Bhandar, and Raigad Bazaar, were all run by co-operatives.

On that warm October afternoon as the fan cooled a dimly lit Raigad Bazaar, we both kept absorbing the buzzing setup, observing its shoppers, staff, standing behind checkouts to see what people were buying and watching several husbands and wives, as they pushed trolleys through the aisles, eavesdropping on some of their talk. The self-service store had basic racks and mostly standard grocery products. For the just liberalising small-town India, the product range was reasonably large and modern. Four girls were ringing sales on cash registers and there were atleast five people standing in each queue. The store offered minor discounts on some of the products and there were a couple of nice promotional campaigns running there.

Alibaug is a small farmer-trader petty-industry town with a modest population. Men and women didn't shop for groceries together, in such places. But here they were, mostly couples. They were both involved, checking-out new products and indulging in small conversations with each other before deciding upon every new thing to add to their cart or choosing a larger pack.

'Look, these are not average Alibaug folks. Women are better dressed and all men here are wearing shirts and trousers. They are white collared people—the likes of bank officers, factory supervisors and teachers,' I whispered to my companion.

'And besides their normal groceries, they are all buying newly launched products based on impulse too,' added Damani.

'This is not merely grocery shopping,' I mumbled aloud to my friend. 'Coming to a self-service store with your husband/wife, is a modern thing to do. Buying nice and new simple things for the family and saving a little money in the process, is a nice thing to do together on a Sunday.'

As we walked out of the store we concluded, people were shopping for modernity and not merely groceries at Raigad Bazaar! 'If this is so apparent in dusty Alibaug, it sounds to me like a bumper formula for Mumbai and the suburbs. There's something here,' said Damani, as we got into my car and drove off.

The next few months were spent around Sahakari

Bhandar of Colaba, Apna Bazaar of Parel, KD's at Versova in Mumbai and several ideation and expansion sessions at the quiet corner of the cafe at Ritz Hotel in Churchgate.

For Damani, it became a business model, a plan, and for me, a full-blown addiction. Observing people keenly and endlessly in the marketplace and working hard to decode the underlying drivers of their consumer behaviour.

But it didn't start for me at Raigad Bazaar. I was first sweptoff my feet by my modern retail passion, many continents away in Sao Paulo, Brazil, a couple of years before my life-changing walk around Raigad Bazaar. Back then, I was a brand manager at Hindustan Unilever. For training and projects, we were sent to various markets overseas by Unilever. On one such project to study a Lever Brothers' brand Brillianto in Brazil, I ended up in Sao Paulo, the commercial capital of Brazil. Sao Paulo, though only a shade more developed than Mumbai, had many large hypermarkets, unlike Mumbai. Before this trip, I had seen modern stores only in the European and U.S. context and thought of them as a developed country phenomenon. In the local hypermarkets in Brazil, women shoppers came in buses and were being dropped home by open-top shuttles run by the store, with their shopping bags. The stores were big and full of simple people of limited means. However, the product choice was large and the atmosphere was boisterous and cheerful, like our market places back home.

While I didn't understand the language, I enjoyed watching people shop and decoding their family size and composition based on the mix of products in their trolleys. On our trips to various stores in Sao Paulo, I got my Brazilian colleagues Sam and Julia to play this 'guess family-type from trolley' game with me. After our guesses were done, they would ask the customer a couple of questions and give me a decoding score!

So, even two years before the afternoon at Raigad Bazaar, the 'observe and decode' bug had bitten me. I came back from Sao Paulo, convinced that modern retail in India would flourish soon and some day I'd be part of the phenomenon.

Back then in the MNC marketing world (even now in most cases) decoding consumer behaviour was a task that depended heavily on elaborate market research projects and specialist agencies. The process was rigorous and insights were compared with well established norms and benchmarks. The shopping process was also very opaque and non-revealing of the consumer choice dynamics. The buying-choice influencers for simple home goods happened at home. In the shop, women just went with a list and the list was serviced. The only real change in choice was if the shopkeeper had the time and motivation to recommend a product to the customer.

In the decade following 2000, two things have happened simultaneously in India. One, growing consumer income, aspiration and explosion of choice in the market has given rise to continuously changing purchase behaviour for all families. From food to furniture, we are using very different things from what we did ten years ago. Two, we are buying things very differently than we did, before. Open format, self-service shops is the new way in which many of us increasingly shop for clothes, televisions, noodles, or vegetables.

In this new theatre of self-service shopping in India, with

my hobby to observe and decode consumers, I have had a feast in recent years. For all of us marketers, the Indian customer is a rapidly moving target that needs to be tracked real time.

In India, we have always led much more 'open' lives. Our sense of privacy is easygoing compared to most western societies. We easily talk to and share our feelings with family, friends, neighbours, and even strangers. I have found, talking to people in the marketplace freely, in addition to avidly observing them, keeps me ahead in the interpretation game, as a marketer.

Supermarketwala is the collection of many such decoding stories triggered by my store and market walks providing a unique peep into Indian customers' homes, kitchens, and motives. My job at India's premier retailer Future Group got me to surround myself with a team of designers, sociologists, anthropologists, and market researchers. My insights and interpretations have been validated and strengthened by the inimitable discovery process we developed over the years. We kept journeying through modern and traditional markets, large and small towns, folks of different communities and classes and the sharp insights kept flowing.

We also discovered that the local consumer's outlook was making a lot of difference to the business and marketing models in the emerging Indian market. Behind each 'ahaa' insight was a way to succeed and make money faster in the Indian market. Anyone thinking of the consumer and wanting to shape businesses that work in India should find the stories in the book charming and extremely useful.

Grab a Ring-Side Seat, Tune in, Listen

THERE IS A NEW game in town—the game of freedom of choice, of 'shoptainment', of open brand-flirting and of savings as a participative sport. Women and families are enthusiastically joining this game. In the good old world of over-the-counter shopping, the little things that happen between desire and purchase had a certain mystique. All you got to see was the final purchase. In this new, self-service world there is a bagful of new things, visible like never before.

However, like in a live cricket match, for the sport of shopping you need to know the best angle of view and tune in all your senses to observe and enjoy this new game in town—self-service shopping!

I am going to share things I learnt, by relentlessly walking stores and standing alongside smart retail pioneers like R.K. Damani of D-Mart and Kishore Biyani of Big Bazaar fame. We would walk through our stores, competitions' stores, street markets, or stores on our travels beyond India, all with equal enthusiasm. 'Did you see that…' or 'Why do you think…..', would be the two most frequent questions heard on such occasions. There is a lot to be observed, understood, and decoded just by walking around. Gradually, I made this my own personal habit. I think any retailer will enjoy it when s/he also adopts this habit!

Merely walking through the store and observing customers are two completely different things. Most of us walk through the stores. Moving through sections and aisles swiftly, forming impressions, observing upkeep, displays, promotions, and staff activity. To me, this is nice and necessary, if it is part of my job. But seeing the store in this manner is the cricket equivalent of observing the stadium, the sight screen, the pitch conditions, and the outfield. Everything is very important, but that's not the game! When we watch the game, we need to slow down, be still, let the stadium fade out into a blur and focus patiently on the players—the bowling action, the footwork of the batsman, the movement of the fielder. In the same manner, in a store, we need to focus on the customer, her movement, trolley, and bags! You can't rush this. Our pace has to slow down to the customer's pace. The most prized angle of view, when you want a feel for the entire store and its meaning for the customer, is just behind the check-out counter of the store. Stand there for a few minutes every time you are at a store, slow down, scan the contents of the trolleys and body language of customers. I do this at every store visit of mine—every time.

When we walk as customers, with customers, we realise customers are after all, people! They behave, you'll notice, like people. In India, they walk on the left; they speed up in straight, empty aisles; they slow down when they have to go round a bin or a stack full of goods. The store gains when customers slow down and loses when they walk straight through. People can't help stopping at mirrors; children will insist on going to a section with funny concave mirrors in the corner. People can't resist stepping onto a free weighing scale in a remote corner of the store. If a narrow aisle with tall racks is over 16 ft long without a break or a turn, people feel 'tunnelled and claustrophobic'. When you walk just behind a customer, at her speed, some of these things will spring up as obvious. At the same time, they are critical to the way retailers design store layouts. When we feel it, sense it, we'll do something about it.

As retailers, we want customers to stroll at a slow pace, go to all parts of our store, feel positive and have their guard down when they are in our aisles. Many small things help ensure this. Come to think of it, done this way, it is quite simple, isn't it? But most retail managers do not do it!

Men and women shop quite differently. Take apparel shopping, for instance. Their differences are stark when buying clothes. For example, if a man takes a shirt to the trial room, there is a two-third probability he'll buy some shirt at the store, on this visit. With a woman, it is less than one-fourth the chance! In supermarkets or apparel stores in India the time spent in the store (and therefore money spent) is highest when two women come to shop together. Next, a woman alone, then a woman and a man together, and the worst—a man, alone! In an electronics or a home goods store, men are in their element and can be very good for business, when alone!

The self-service store, in many ways, is quite 'transparent'. If we stand near a shelf, stop, and just watch what the customer looks at, touches, picks up and buys or rejects on the shelf, we can almost spell out what's going on in her mind. The customer decision-tree is apparent provided we look for it. I find most customers are open to changing their minds at the shelf, just moments before the actual purchase. If we observe and know how this works for our category of items, we can trigger a switch to a bigger pack or a comparable brand by merely modifying our display and stacking logically on the shelf.

Each one of us, as retail managers and marketers, has different grasp levels and working preferences that we shall deploy to take us from 'walking through stores' to 'observing the shopping game'. My personal favourite method is keeping a deliberate customer time, at every store visit. That's when I slow down to the speed of the customer or just stand still and observe for an extended period from one place. Observing trolleys and not shelves is another habit I find handy. And here is a slightly risky but powerful method—if the customer is god, god's voice can only be heard by those who wear the uniform. It may make you look silly at times, since you may not know the nuances of the store as much as the regular store associates. But never mind that—for me, what you get to hear in the uniform, you can never hear wearing a boss' tie. It's worth a try!

☛ MIND POKE

The global pioneer in in-store ethnography is a gentleman called Paco Underhill. Read his book, '*Why we Buy*?' I am a fan of Paco's methods of customer observation. I, however, sometimes question applicability of his universal principles in the Indian stores of today. One such example is, in the Elbow Push Factor chapter ahead in the book.

PART 1

LIFESTYLES

The New Temples of Democracy

INDIA HAS BEEN A democracy for over sixty years and proudly wears the crown of being the world's largest one. In such a deep rooted democracy, it would be natural for us to expect civic life where just being a citizen of the nation would be enough qualification for us to be welcome and be served in any public location. After all non-discrimination and equality for all citizens is enshrined in our constitution. Every institution, whether in the public or private sphere, is supposed to respect that. However, all through history, equality has never been part of our social and cultural genes. We have always existed with the concept of inequality and privilege for a few. The Constitution of India, a well-drafted document, which has taken precedents from the best laws from across the world, has had insufficient impact on our deep-rooted superstitious beliefs and practices. Therefore, in most cases, while equality is intended, it's not delivered in practice. From schools to places of worship, from social ceremonies to urban clubs, from police stations to government offices, we come across access control by design or by informal practices that keep a certain set of people 'out'. This has been the traditional mindset of both the privileged and the deprived, with the latter mostly accepting that they do not have the right to enter such institutions.

Modern Retail Is Inclusive

However, can we say that some noticeable change in this mindset is happening? The harbingers of this change are our very own malls, hypermarts and supermarkets. In urban India, these are rapidly emerging as public places that have no discrimination of any kind built into their design or practice. Most of the time, being a human is enough to be allowed in—if you can go to a public park in India, you can get into a mall—caste, creed, dress code, membership, gender, even economic status hold no bar! As opposed to traditional institutions, the institutions of modern retail are designed to be inclusive and welcoming. In the early days, a mall in Mumbai tried to keep out 'undesirable people' and suffered a huge negative backlash. Though commercial entities, they have become public spaces and even if one buys nothing, one gets to be in the comfortable, air-conditioned surroundings, with clean flooring, good toilets, bright lighting, and pleasant, positive imagery surrounding their senses. Where else can one experience these comforts in India, other than in the super expensive and exclusive luxury hotels? The only truly public places like beaches and parks are perpetually dirty and badly maintained, and do not welcome so much as repel. Most people visit these places because there is no alternative available. The new malls now provide an alternative far superior in quality but equally, if not more, accessible in design.

If universal franchise—the principle of one person one vote—is the cornerstone of our democratic institutions, then 'One person, unlimited aspirations' is the cornerstone of the new economic resurgence of our society. And this resurgence is here to stay. There can be no going back on the path of modernization. And 'have aspiration, shall be served' has to be the credo of the new marts—the new temples of our democracy.

As an individual, I can truly discover freedom in these new temples. So far that was not the case. Access to new, innovative products and services, as well as competitive price deals were all along the privilege of the rich, even in urban India. Modern retail has reversed this trend. The malls have truly democratized the choices and prices available to the common man. As a part of the urban middle-class, I now matter, even my customs are important to the shopkeepers. In my buying process too, I have discovered the freedom to browse and window-shop without a shopkeeper assessing every move of mine, including my purchasing power and trying to advise me on what's good for me. I have a mind of my own and am happy to enjoy freedom from the influence of traditional shopkeepers who always seemed to know more than me.

In the old days only Bollywood and television catered to the entertainment needs of every individual in India, irrespective of class. In that sense these are truly democratic institutions, both in their content and their availability. Any class of person is welcome inside a cinema hall and can watch a film catering to his sensibilities. Television subscribes to no shibboleths and talks of issues that are of significance to everyone. But in that world, I am the passive spectator. The stars are on the screen and I just sit there admiring them and buying the dreams they sell. I cannot participate. However, in the new malls, I am on the centre stage and the rest of the world is there to serve me. I have the power and I live, play, and actively enjoy the experience.

Task Ahead

The task for all current and future mall owners and new retailers is to protect and build on the sheer democratic design of these new temples. This will need extra effort. There is a fundamental difference between the shopkeepers of yesterday and today. In the 'small shop' days, the small shopkeeper and the shopper were from the same strata of society and it was easy to stay in tune with the shoppers' needs. The shopkeepers knew what the customer wanted because that's mostly what even his wife wanted. And his shop stocked accordingly. In contrast, the big shopkeepers of today are rich individuals or large companies that don't have any real time contact with the customer and are prone to make mistakes in recognizing his/her needs. This is a delicate issue. There are tools to handle these things, market research for instance, but there's no substitute for direct contact. Mall owners and shopkeepers will succeed when they tune their merchandise and outlook to what the modern urban shopper is looking for. There will always be business opportunity in the super premium segments of retailing, for some businesses. However, the impact on the society at large will be created by those from this breed that choose the path that touches more lives of the 'middle-class India'. Those who can connect with the large consuming class and help them shed the inhibition of trying out the modern, empowering way to shop, will, apart from building large businesses, contribute to our democratic ethos as well.

And those who venture out beyond large towns and into the hinterland will truly be pioneers, for that's where democracy, choice and access will impact lives most.

In the last ten years, aspirations have been firmly democratized. The customer 'God' is definitely middle-class now. The retail fraternity has to keep making sure that these temples welcome and serve the new gods well.

The socially inclusive ethos of modern retail has led to another phenomenon that might, justifiably, be called the festivals of democracy. If festivals are markers of celebration, then in multicultural India, they are also visible signboards of segregation. Abida knows that it is only a rare Hindu who will visit her during Eid, and she in turn has never been invited to a Diwali gathering at her Hindu neighbor's place. Regardless of the pomp and ceremony associated with these festivals, regardless of the message of harmony and goodwill that they are supposed to communicate, festivals are inclusive only when they add commercial values to their aura. Thus, Christmas in India is remembered more for the discount sales that stores hold, than for its Christian spirit. People like to be respected for who they are, not what they should be, and the democratic ethos of stores ensures that each person is respected, if only as a customer. The air of celebration and festivity attendant upon every event in a store, whether it is a weekly sale or a season sale, the enthusiasm with which customers respond to the call of these 'festivals', the sense of participation and cheer that they engender, and the egalitarian philosophy of competing with everyone to get the best bargains, turn a store event into a festival of sorts, albeit a secular one.

Once upon a time, festivals and temples distinguished

between castes and communities—the haves and have nots. And other social and civic institutions followed suit. That story was bound to have a sad ending. The world of free commerce opens doors for so many more people to feel wanted and included. Surely that's a good thing and must be encouraged.

MIND POKE

Growing up, the only truly inclusive experience full of general bonhomie and sharing I remember, was the long train journeys one undertook once a year. Does any other inclusive experience come to mind?

Tell us on the Supermarketwala Facebook page. Please scan the QR Code using your smartphones to take you directly to the Facebook site.

Shopkeeper-in-law

WHEN RITA JOSHI, A suburban housewife from Mumbai, visits a neighbourhood supermarket, it is doubtful if she's thinking about how she's benefiting the potato farmers of Punjab by doing so. Her concerns are more pedestrian. Is she getting what she wants at a good price? Is the produce fresh? Does the store stock everything that she is likely to need for her family of four? Can she hire an auto to take her back home when she's done shopping? Rita also has other concerns on her mind, concerns that she might find embarrassing and awkward to share with anyone else. Does the store offer the brand of sanitary napkins that she has recently switched to, after seeing it advertised on television? Can she buy a newly introduced beauty soap for herself without anyone else being wiser about it? Rita is quite sure that what she chooses to buy is no one's business except her own.

Unfortunately for her, so far, society hasn't always seen it like that. If asked, Rita wouldn't be able to articulate why exactly she is determined to shop at the supermarket in preference to the neighbourhood kirana store. She just knows that even though her old grocer delivers at home, in contrast to the supermarket to which she has to take an auto, she would still much rather go there than continue to patronise the former. Of course, she enjoys the variety and discounts that the supermarket offers, but she is also shrewd enough to understand on the whole, in spite of the discounts and offers, her monthly grocery bill remains unchanged. In fact, it might even have gone up slightly, courtesy the little knick-knacks that she almost always ends up buying on impulse. Nonetheless, Rita, who was originally a sceptic, has now become a true blue convert to modern retail. Though Rita doesn't know why she shifted from her traditional grocer to the gigantic supermarket, we do.

One of the most interesting aspects of modern retail is its potential for social transformation. In the normal buzz about supermarkets in India, where the focus is usually on either their frequent sales or their impact on the friendly neighbourhood kirana stores, this role of modern retail is lost or blurred. We don't think about how a different shopping habit can actually change the personality of the customer, and therefore, society at large, whereas we should. Why has Rita embraced a large, anonymous, unfamiliar shopping experience so enthusiastically even though her wallet isn't richer? In point of fact, this angle will have a more far-reaching effect on the desire for modern retail than any perceived bargains. As students of retail, therefore, it is our responsibility to highlight this contribution of modern retail and celebrate it.

Though it is important to talk about retail-square feet and employment figures, we cannot neglect the customer side of the story. Does the customer think about the impact on the farmer when she enters a store? Of course not. Cynics might highlight her fondness for a good bargain. But as Rita tells us, that's not what modern retail is about. Then why does Rita go there?

In the nineteenth century, French novelist Emile Zola wrote a book called *Au Bonheur des Dames*. The crux of this well known novel was that women flock to places that can offer them a good bargain. In a time of uncertainty and strife the department store, Au Bonheur des Dames, succeeds because it offers superior merchandise at a price that no small shop can offer. Zola got the story right only partially. Perhaps at the time when he wrote the book, modern retail in the present self-service format hadn't been thought of. Today, the success of modern retail is no longer only a function of discounts and sales. There's another significant factor that we need to take into account.

Yes, customers welcome bargains and the feeling of having triumphed over the shopkeeper. It makes them feel good to know that they are winning over the retailer, even if that's not necessarily true. But what customers value even more in an urban context is anonymity. Anonymity is not only about knowing one's name. There are many other pieces of information that a customer would prefer not to keep in the public domain. Is this possible in the traditional trade? Rita recounts how, when she got married, she came to live with her in-laws. She went shopping where her mother-in-law shopped. The grocer had known the family for more than a quarter of a century, and was familiar with all their preferences. Now with the induction of a new member, he made it his business to know her preferences as well. Though it was nice to be greeted by name every time Rita visited the store, very soon she discovered that she found the grocer's familiarity with her buying habits intrusive. Her preferences, her shopping habits, what she buys and how she buys it, all this is information that the customer would much prefer not telling anyone else about, especially her local grocer. She doesn't wish to be assessed, merely served. And yet, across most neighbourhoods in India, that's exactly what she is subjected to.

A large research project by the Universities of Surrey and Exeter in the UK studying shopping in post-war (1950-70) England, in the sunrise days of modern retail there, discovered that supermarkets were welcomed more by younger and middle-class women. 'It was upper-class matrons, the sort who dressed up to go shopping, who missed the personal attention shown by traditional grocers.' The project quotes a retired secretary recalling, as a young bride, asking the butcher for a small amount of 'premium' mince meat. 'Oh, having a dinner party, madam?' sneered the shopkeeper. This wasn't uncommon. A woman buying anything expensive or unusual risked gossip spread by the shop assistant.

So how does grocery shopping in India look from the perspective of young and middle-class women? A significant clue lies in the manner in which the young bahu addresses the grocer. It is with the same respect that she would use with a senior member of the family. 'Panditji, Guptaji, Anna, Gauru, or Bhaisaheb', are the norm! Just like Rita called him 'Uncle'. After all, the family grocer is friendly with the father-in-law and the mother-in-law. He is one of them, older, more knowledgeable, more moneyed, and safely sitting behind the counter, while the 'bahu' customer is outside, often on the street. Most of the time, the fan is directed on him, and the customer has to sweat it out at the counter. She might be giving him her custom but he is the one patronising her. It is a position of disempowerment for the customer, especially the young, recently married woman, who is still feeling her way about.

Now imagine if she asks Panditji for an expensive conditioner that her family has never used, or even worse, for Whisper Ultra Heavy Flow! It's not going to happen.She is supposed to be the customer, the queen, but she is in an awkward social position and in her eyes, and possibly in his as well, he is the powerful 'Shopkeeper-in-Law'.

How do women deal with such familiarity? In most cities and even middle class localities in metros, women don't buy their personal products from the neighbourhood grocery shops. They buy them when they go out of town or to other neighbourhoods. This is the only way they can retain their anonymity. It is not too far-fetched to suggest that the neighbourhood grocer, for whom confidentiality is an alien value, would be only too happy to discuss a young woman's purchases, especially if they involve something new, with the rest of her family. And she knows that, and is uncomfortable with that.

In India, women have to buy all they need, all their life, from men, often from men with a tendency and licence to intrude, comment, assess, and advise. The new supermarkets zap these men away from between the woman shopper and her choices. Let's see how. A woman feels like trying out Dove soap, instead of her family's normal Lux or Hamam. She picks up a bar of Dove, smells it, sees the price, is shocked at the premium and simply puts it back and chooses another soap. This process of discovering new products and their acceptance or rejection happens comfortably, without any social embarrassment or sneering by shop assistants. It is even more apparent when she is looking for personal hygiene products, items that are freely advertised on TV but then recede to the inner shelves of a grocery store, only to emerge if the customer asks for them, an uncomfortable and eyebrow raising moment. The woman's comfort with her own sense of aspiration, and discomfort with someone else's possible disapproval, propels her to the self-service format. She doesn't want anyone to come between her and her choices. In a way she knows that the 'help' that a grocer offers comes at a price—loss of freedom. That's why young and middle-class women are increasingly voting with their wallets in favour of supermarkets. The friendly, trusted family grocer is trusted only for the elders in the family, people who are used to help in decision-making. He doesn't share the same camaraderie with the younger recruits. In fact, he suffers an emphatic setback every time a new daughter-in-law is added to this customer's household. The trusted family grocer stands for everything that a young woman would be happy without, familiarity and superiority.

This compelling angle of female empowerment is often missing in the supermarket vs kirana debate. In my view, the real trouble for the 'counter service' stores is going to be at the hands of young women, more than anything else. No wonder the Surrey and Exeter study discovered press advertisements from the early days promoting not just the convenience of supermarkets but also their anonymity!

With growing household incomes, more awareness, widening aspirations, we are perpetually trying and buying new products, different from what we bought last month. This sense of freedom is hampered if there's someone looking over our shoulder, constantly assessing our purchases, and through those, our social aspirations. We certainly don't wish to be asked if we are having a party at home!

MIND POKE

Take a little risk. Chat with a young daughter-in-law who lives in a joint family, about her store and shopping preferences.

Tell us on the Supermarketwala Facebook page. Please scan the QR Code using your smartphones to take you directly to the Facebook site.

Ten Days of India Two

SHANTA TAI LIVES IN a hovel by the side of P. D'Mello Marg in Mumbai. There is about a foot of space between it and the road, one of the busiest arteries in Mumbai. Her four children face death from a speeding truck for 355 days in a year. On the other ten days, the neighbourhood Ganesh Utsav committee stakes out a piece of the road for its festivities. During that time, no vehicle can come within ten feet of Shanta Tai's hovel, which is transformed into a safe home. To top it all, there is an air of gaiety and colour during the festival with the garishly done up *pandal* that is placed firmly on the road, and it is no wonder that all of the children's time is spent frolicking in the technicolour marquee where they play fearlessly. During the rest of the year, there is no question of the children being able to play anywhere without risking their lives. There is no place.

On the tenth day, the deity is sent back to his heavenly abode with much fanfare by his devotees, including dancing in the streets, heedless of the endless lines of stalled traffic that surround them.

What is true for the roads during the festival is true for the festival itself. What was once the bastion of the middle-class has now got infiltrated by the deprived classes, whose manner of offering prayer and collective merrymaking is totally at variance from the past. The prayers are louder, the entertainment is more popular culture, and Bollywood song and dance routines have replaced chaste, one-act plays. The dancers and marchers who imperiously halt traffic to give way to their own Ganpati almost seem to make a statement. And that is this is *their* time, when they will lay claim to the mostly unreachable physical and social infrastructure of the city.

The uneven pace of development in India has ensured that a small part of the population, the middle-class, has claimed the lion's share of the country's infrastructure. Nowhere is this more obvious than in the metropolises, where squatter settlements housing ten people in a ten by ten foot dwelling stand next to luxurious high rise apartment buildings. Chauffeur driven cars zoom past the notorious local trains filled to four times their capacity on a good day. The poor, for all their numbers, might as well be invisible. Shanta Tai has no access to formal housing, in spite of having lived in the city for close to two decades. Nothing in the city indicates that there is some thought devoted to the comfort of people mostly existing at subsistence level. The lives of the poor are perpetually threatened and circumscribed by the limitations of ever shrinking urban infrastructure. The middle-class ignores the deprived classes, and there's almost complete disregard for their welfare, except when its lack affects their own lives.

However, not all is lost for the deprived when it comes to assertion of one's existence. Religious festivals willingly accommodate the biggest power they have, the power of numbers. Be it Ganesh Chaturthi, Mumbai's famous

Govinda festival, Durga Puja in the East or Ramlila in the North, be it the celebrations of Id-e-Milad or the annual Bandra Fair of Mount Mary, it is the economically ignored who come out in hordes to support these occasions. Roads, electricity for the *pandals*, and public space are all at their disposal, unlike during the rest of the year when only the well-heeled can claim ownership.

Wherever there is true exercise of democracy, the deprived elbow out the middle-class. The middle-class complains bitterly of its irrelevance at election time, but this is true even on other occasions. Even a mega-sale at a hypermarket will see *chawl* dwellers turn out in large numbers and hog all the available space. They will gather their friends and neighbours and place them strategically inside the store to get hold of the best bargains before stocks run out, they will willingly stand in line in the hot sun, patiently awaiting their turn to enter the overcrowded store. So, while on non-sale days, the middle-class denizens of the neighbourhood have the run of the store, at the time of a sale, it is their deprived and otherwise feeble counterparts who move in. Clever stores that are marketing-savvy choose to stock merchandise—big packs of snacks and cold drinks, low-end non-stick ware, irons and phones, synthetic carpets, LCD television sets, low cost jeans, etc.—that appeals to this class of customers during their megasales, and not just things that are consumed by the more affluent classes. In their own way, retailers are feeding the aspirations of the have-nots and partnering with them in their urge to grow and progress, unlike the state that continues to frown upon consumerism as a vehicle for progress. The telecom companies were in the vanguard of this approach. With their ultra-cheap packages, they ensured that every Indian could access a communication device, and fuel her own aspiration. Migrant labour, the working backbone of any city, is able to keep in touch with developments back home using this device. The upside of this phenomenon is the spread of consumerism through the ripple effect. The migrant takes to the village his experiences in the city, and lo and behold! A new trend is created.

Be it reality shows like *Indian Idol* or competition sports like cricket that make heroes out of ordinary people, wherever determined effort and patience are rewarded, the masses are edging out the classes visibly. In the democratic set up offered by these events, there is no place for the regime of privilege that the Indian middle-class has thrived upon for so long. The private enterprise urge to open access to the largest possible group gives India Two a great opportunity to exercise the power of numbers.

Unlike the socialist era, in the new economic surge, the aspiring classes are seeing a new world, one where it is all right to have desires since there is some possibility that they shall be met. With such a mindset, the middle class no longer holds a monopoly over the country's resources. The growth of media and the Internet brings social dynamics into every person's life, and in spite of a marginalized existence, there's hardly a man or woman on the street who doesn't understand the potential of consumerism, for instance. The visibility of India Two of Shanta Tai is only going to increase. Its numbers and rising aspirations will ensure that it edges out the India One of the middle class. City planners and community leaders will have to learn to accommodate this reality in their thinking and living. The definition of 'civilised' for India is changing, and Shanta Tai is showing us that.

MIND POKE

Next time there is a big Republic Day or Independence Day sale, go into a popular big store and look for folks who would not be regular shoppers at such stores. Observe them. Share with us the interesting stories you come across.

Tell us on the Supermarketwala Facebook page. Please scan the QR Code using your smartphones to take you directly to the Facebook site.

Stop! Uniforms Ahead

PUJA PANCHAL IS TWENTY eight and works as a railway ticket clerk. Her husband, Vinod, is a driver in South Mumbai. Puja and Vinod live with Vinod's parents and their eight year old son in a chawl in Mulund, a suburb in northeast Mumbai. Every Sunday, the couple visits the local mall, and buys their groceries from the supermarket there. Once in a while, Vinod's parents accompany them on the excursion. Though not happily.

Vinod's father, Sharad Pandurang Panchal, or Sharad Kaka (Uncle), as he's popularly called, is a fitter at a factory near his home. There are a number of shops in that neighbourhood, part of a fairly large and well-stocked market, and Sharad Kaka is used to frequenting those shops, and not the mall. Consider Sharad Kaka's journey in the mall. As he enters, there's a uniformed guard waiting to frisk him. Once he's in, there's another man in uniform at the bottom of the escalator. At the entrance to the store, there's yet another security guard inspecting Sharad Kaka's bags, and 'confiscating' them while he shops. At the exit, there's another uniform to check his bill. For just one simple visit to a store, Sharad Kaka encounters four uniformed people. It is enough to deter him from shopping in the mall.

'I feel guilty, as though I've done something wrong,' he says, when asked about his reluctance to shop at the mall. In his mind, far from protecting him, the uniformed guards seem to threaten him, as though they're there to check him and snoop on him. He doesn't view them as his protectors, but his challengers. 'You never know,' he explains, 'when you could get into trouble with one of these guys.' Uniformed people, explained the man, almost always meant trouble for simple folk like him. He said firmly that men in uniform were there to make sure that the customers didn't make mischief and so were best avoided by innocent people like him. Puja and Vinod, for whom the mall is a huge blessing, don't share this opinion. They've grown up in a different era, one where they're no longer cowed down by the appearance of authority. In the new India of loud media and Twitter, almost everything can be questioned and challenged. For them, in fact, the uniforms are a blessing. These represent system and organization, and offer a sort of reassurance that nothing much can be wrong in a world where there's so much vigilance.

When his wife talks of the various bargains brought back by the neighbours from these new fangled places, Sharad Kaka does not deny it. He has heard others extol the virtues of the large open spaces, the closed circuits cameras, the shopping trolleys, the background music, but he is adamant in his refusal to go into these hypermarkets that he passes everyday on his way to work. He claims he is not wanted. He has seen the burly security guards manning the entrances to these stores. When someone wants to enter the store, he is actually turned away to another counter, to deposit his belongings. 'How,' asks Sharad Kaka, 'will I manage to take my necessary *pishwi* (the little bag) inside the store? Are we all shoplifters?' he asks. Certainly he isn't one and doesn't want to go inside a store where he might be caught on the wrong foot for no fault of his.

In his own kirana store, by contrast, Sharad Kaka is known and treated with trust. He can browse around, pick up things and put them back, and there are no security guards or closed circuit cameras watching every move he makes. When he leaves, there is nobody checking his bill, another act that makes him feel vaguely guilty. He knows that the larger stores probably offer some very good deals on the things he buys, but he still prefers shopping at the local kirana store.

The overall security environment in all large stores, to Sharad Kaka, signifies a stand in for policing. As a man living in a worker environment, he has enough of that without it encroaching on his shopping life, as well! Even within a large store, there are men and women in uniform who appear to be patrolling the aisles all the time, keeping a watch on what one is up to. This, to Sharad Kaka, and millions of others like him, is an intrusion into his private space, a space that he guards jealously since it is so hard-won.

Security means different things to different people. Therefore, though on the one hand it could be a reassuring symbol of safety to middle class housewives, to people like Sharad Kaka and millions like him, it is seen as a threat, an invasion into their private space. Large stores must address this issue if they have to attract customers like Sharad Kaka who are, in fact, a very large percentage of the population. It is when these stores actually decide to go to the customer, seek him out in his own milieu, that they can learn to break the class barrier.

A recent heavy bargain sale at one of the leading retail chains in the country is a case in point. The message was loud and clear. Such a good bargain would not be available anywhere. Sharad Kaka was practically dragged to the sale by his wife. There, he found many other people standing in snaking queues that reminded him of the long queue outside Siddhivinayak Temple. The crowds, the chaos, the lack of control, the appearance of a system under stress, all these brought the store closer to Sharad Kaka, for whom such a life is the norm. The harassed security system on such a high footfall day, also offered reassurance to Sharad Kaka that here he was not really being singled out for attention. And of course, the bargains were unbelievable, as Sharad Kaka didn't stop telling everyone around him. Imagine getting a pressure cooker for four hundred rupees!

Large retailers need to develop models for getting close to people like Sharad Kaka. Spic and span stores, glitzy surroundings, English speaking personnel and above all, the security and the uniformed staff, obviously don't seem to do it. The unfamiliarity of this format, its association with authoritarianism and policing, turns away many people who would actually stand to benefit from the many sales on offer at any point in a modern store, sales that can be far richer in quality compared to the normal kirana store.

While the mall management will obviously have to apply security measures, the days of easy access to public spaces being behind us forever, there are many steps that can be taken to give the modern mall a more inclusive look. In India malls are urban paradoxes, huge structures in space deprived metros. Their size can be used to advantage with the community. Are there many places that are available to morning walkers, for instance? Only the elite now have large, open spaces for exercising. Malls can become stand-ins for parks and host community activities.

A survey of what's most important to Sharad Kaka and people like him in their daily life would reveal that their morning prayers are indispensable. Can malls offer a small, silent place of worship next to a puja shop? Visually, won't it send out a signal that malls aren't simply places of idle entertainment for the young, but are sensitive to what the entire community requires?

In their appearance, there's something synthetic about every mall. The same lighting, the same shopping, the same aura of antiseptic organization. Indians have always shopped in bazaars. Once in a while, why can't malls replicate the bazaar ambience? A weekly farmer's market, for instance, where things are sold from carts by the farmers themselves, and all transactions are in the local language. How reassuring it would be to Sharad Kaka to know that his familiarity with chaos is valued, and not dismissed with contempt.

There are many things that modern retail can do to reach out to the larger community instead of just the demographic of the top five per cent of the population. A beginning needs to be made.

MIND POKE

In general, women actually find malls safer than the streets. Everyone entering there is frisked, watched, and is therefore on good behavior. Different strokes for different folks?

Tell us on the Supermarketwala Facebook page. Please scan the QR Code using your smartphones to take you directly to the Facebook site.

Unexpected Ripples: Modern Retail Touches More Lives Than You Think

Bringing up brother, with lessons in store

RAGHAVAN, A DEPARTMENT MANAGER in an upmarket store in Mumbai, was a bit intrigued when an elderly lady walked up to him one day and said, 'You have changed our entire family for the better. Please do visit us at home.' The woman was, Raghavan discovered, one of his customer associate, Sulekha's mother. Sulekha works in the men's-casuals section of the store. Raghavan recruited her two years ago from a bank of resumes that landed on his desk when the job was advertised. Sulekha's main qualification was that she had worked in a clothing store before, though not in a modern retail format. It wasn't exactly relevant experience but it was the best on offer. Ideally, Raghavan would have liked a person with modern retail experience. There was a difference, though Raghavan couldn't pinpoint what. He was about to find out.

A few days later, as promised, Raghavan went for a courtesy visit to Sulekha's place, located two kilometers from the store, in a modest chawl. She lived there with her parents and two brothers.

'Her father works in a small factory in MIDC. Her bhau (elder brother) drives an auto,' said the mother, referring to Sulekha's father and brother, as Raghavan sipped tea. 'And this brat here, Suresh, is the youngest, in sixth standard.'

After keenly listening to Sulekha's mother for half an hour, the full depth of her 'changed our entire family' statement unfolded in Raghavan's mind. He had a hint of the difference that modern retail made in shaping the lives of people.

The interactions and atmosphere in Sulekha's family were earlier defined by the influences the father and the elder brother brought from their work environments—a small factory floor and the streets of the city, respectively. And everyone in the neighbourhood inhabits a similar world. The language there is rough and tough, expletives are commonplace and everyone tends to get aggressive at the slightest pretext. Alcohol consumption is fairly regular and women often face aggression at home. The environment is the typical industrial era environment, male dominated and coarse. A certain amount of aggression is almost necessary in a factory.

In the service industry, aggression is the last thing an employee needs. The store where Sulekha works knows this. Every employee in Raghavan's organization has to undergo a 'Gurucool' induction week upon joining, where the main emphasis is on inculcating self belief, confidence, gender equality, and soft skills. Of course, a certain amount of unlearning is involved. Many of the recruits hail from tough, industrial backgrounds, and soft skills are not something they've seen in their own life. Now Raghavan knew why so many trainees found 'GuruCool' life changing. Confidence in self, respect for others, listening, firm but polite talk were indeed things that were very different from the family context they had hitherto experienced.

On the modern retail floor, 60 per cent of employees are women and no one dares treat them with disrespect. 'Even customers, when they come to malls, seem to behave better,' girls often said, in team meetings. 'Sir, that smart uniform of yours is like armour for my Sulekha,' her mother said. 'She can talk to anyone, as high a position as they may be in, when she has the uniform on!'

As far as self-confidence and egalitarianism on the shop floor is concerned, though modern retail employees on the floor are often only high school graduates, they are given intense technical training about the products in their section. For instance, the young male associate in the international branded shoes section, though speaking in Hindi, knows more, and talks more confidently about running shoes than any of his customers. And that does a world of good to his self-esteem. It is a pleasure to see young women confidently explaining the features of different types of jeans, and which kind suits the customer best. And through all interactions, these young men and women, who otherwise live in a world of harshness, remain polite and helpful, firm yet friendly.

Before modern stores came into being, what employment options did young boys and girls, with modest education, have near their homes? Tiny, traditional retail stores were crammed places with low pay, no training, no rights, and sweatshop work conditions. Small factories would offer seasonal packing or cleaning jobs to girls like Sulekha. Modern stores, branded restaurants, and chain hotels, on the other hand, are opening up new job opportunities that require hard work but offer a host of 'organized sector' benefits to local youngsters. And gradually the social acceptance of these new job profiles is also changing as urban society accepts the new context in which young Indians are working. One of the early department store leaders, B.S. Nagesh of Shoppers' Stop, once said, 'It was seven long years before our customer care associates were fine going out in store-uniforms after work!'

Today, Sulekha's mom calls the same uniform her 'confidence armour'! While Sulekha's worldview, confidence, and behavior had all changed, that was not the only impact that her new employment situation had. It permeated down to the rest of her family, to what Sulekha inculcated in her kid brother, to how she laid down the law on her 'bhau's' treatment of his wife. The skills that Sulekha learnt at work were now automatically transferred to her domestic environment as well.

'Having a confident youngster—a woman with her own independent opinions, shapes the entire family. She can make us all happier and more optimistic about our future. Thank you for taking our Sulekha and giving us such a nice young woman, Sir,' signed-off her mother, with moist eyes.

This is not a romantic view of modern retail. These swanky modern, corporate stores are changing not just us, the served, but also the lives of those who serve us there. Look for stories of Neha Srivastava from Lucknow and Jyoti Lodhi from Bhopal in the January 20, 2013 edition of the *Indian Express Eye*. Neha worked in a high-street mobile store before shifting jobs to a store in a mall. 'People, when they shop at malls, are better behaved,' is Neha's simple observation.

Call-centre jobs were no software jobs. But they changed many young lives. Retail jobs are local jobs, need basic qualifications, but touch a large number of youngsters and their families, as catalysts of hope and change. Even if these jobs are used by people as an interim stepping-stone in their onward journey of life, these new 'steps' help them stand tall and learn to look at their future in the eye. The professionalism, good manners and product expertise that we encounter in modern retail stores don't just happen. They are a result of training and good corporate practices. When employees find themselves belonging to a world that they had only aspired to in the past, when they are paid a proper salary every month on the same date, when their skills are upgraded periodically, when they have a ladder worth climbing in their work environment, when they interact with customers who are educated and mostly polite, when their workplace is comfortable, not just for their customers, but for them also, when everyone around them speaks the language of 'tehzeeb' which can very loosely be translated as 'politeness', they become what they see.

Try sensing the human story behind the uniformed person when you meet her in the store next time.

☛ MIND POKE

Owner of Shopper's Stop, B.S. Nagesh runs a trust, TRRAIN, which is involved in wide ranging activities including ways to associate greater dignity and pride in being a retail associate by way of training. You can do your bit by logging on to their Facebook page and participating in some of the activities and sharing your experience with us. At Reliance Retail, we employ physically challenged associates, under TRRAIN's guidance. They excel in their work with customers.

Tell us on the Supermarketwala Facebook page. Please scan the QR Code using your smartphones to take you directly to the Facebook site.

Recycling and Modern Retail

100 percent of all newspapers and milk pouches are preserved, reused or sold for recycling in India

REENA JAIN IS A teacher in a private school in Mumbai, and her husband is a banker. Their two children are twelve and ten years old, respectively. Reena prides herself on being a 'modern' woman. Her kitchen is equipped with the latest gizmos, they eat out as often or more than most middle-class families in the city, they see the latest movies that come to town, and they have frequent vacations in India and abroad. Their life is no different from the lives of most middle-class households in Indian metros, down to the little cabinet next to the shoe rack for storing old newspapers. Reena continues to store old clothes, plastic bags, discarded metal fittings, anything that can be given away to the used goods trader, that is, the good old *raddiwala*, who comes round once a month to trade cash for old things. The cash received is insignificant, but Reena can't bring herself round to simply dumping things in the trash. In fact, Reena naturally veers towards 'hoarding'. She collects plastic bags and uses them as dustbin liners, carries her own carry bags for vegetable shopping, and has rarely thrown away worn shoes. Her staff could always do with a pair of shoes, even if they're used.

In the kitchen, Reena is thrift personified. Everything is recycled, reused, refrigerated. Pasta and rice, she has discovered, are easy vehicles for using left overs. There is no space, she claims proudly, for wasting food in her home. Her children are urged to finish everything on their plate, whether at home or in a restaurant. Reena and her husband, Jayesh, supervise mealtimes to ensure that food doesn't go into the dustbin. Leftover food after a big party gets parcelled out to various service providers the next day. Sometimes, when Reena is forced to throw out stale food, she can't help feel a pang of guilt. It seems utterly wasteful to do so.

Reena doesn't give a second thought to all the recycling that she does so naturally. There was a time when, as a child, Reena would get all the blank pages from her used notebooks bound for reuse. Only used pages were discarded, never blank ones. Dresses were never thrown if their hemlines could be let out further. Till the age of twelve Reena wore her sister's old clothes, an indignity that she doesn't inflict upon her own children. Reena has come a long way, but even so thrift and recycling are a way of life, something she has grown up with, a second nature of sorts. She is unaware that she is contributing in any way to helping the environment. It's just how she lives. She doesn't call these activities 'reducing food waste', 'segregating trash for recycle and reuse', 'reducing our carbon footprint', 'green living' and so on.

There's a good reason for this. We don't give these activities any name because they aren't separate from the rest of our lives. Our lives are woven around saving, whether it's money or yesterday's newspaper. These new terms have emerged from the West, where hugely wasteful societies are struggling to change habits and practices as the realisation dawns that we are living on a gradually warming planet, where resources are getting scarcer. In fact, what was once considered natural—throwing away what is not needed—is now recognised and treated as wastefulness. As societies moved to modernity, all extra effort that was not directed towards leisure or work was considered superfluous.

Waste and modernity, therefore, are almost synonymous. Modernity is accompanied by convenience, which is almost always derived from habits that are wasteful. It is easier to throw away what is not required than to engage in another transaction for very small monies. As for food, since it was always plentiful, there seemed no point in compromising on taste or appetite. One simply threw away what one didn't like or couldn't eat. Supermarkets aren't free from guilt either. Stocking up, indulging, experimenting, practically everything was the result of seeing miles of shelves groaning with goods.

Fortunately, in India, we are still not fully 'modern'. We still believe in simple and thrifty living, and don't mind putting in effort to propagate such a lifestyle. But just as Reena forswears from recycling notebooks, a relic from her past, so her children will drop some things that she practices. With the onslaught of new age influences, our children are becoming more and more distant from such habits and consider them old-fashioned and 'fuddy-duddy'. Many times, they're right. Many of the practices are no longer sustainable in their current form. The *raddiwala* is increasingly irrelevant in most households. Organised charities and eBay have replaced this particular transaction.

In the last ten years modernity has wrought many changes in India. Entertainment, telecommunications, holidaying, fashion, retail have all entered a new phase. The old way of doing things in all these sectors has been transformed almost beyond recognition. What does that imply for recycling? Will the traditional ways of handling waste also be simply discontinued as our children enter the modern age? Will they simply dump old newspapers and magazines into the trash? Will garbage dumps now feature all the domestic riff-raff that used to be so carefully sorted out in the old days? If so, will it not be a calamity for India? Pollution is already in the red zone. Discarding the natural tendency towards thrift in favour of a more 'modern' lifestyle will only push us further towards disaster. So what is the solution? Should we simply wring our hands, bemoan the loss of the 'good old days' in an atavistic attempt to remain where we were? Not at all. However, while India has no choice but to embrace modernity, there is a choice we can make to retain some good practices, while integrating them into a modern lifestyle.

Enter modern retail. Modern retail in India has been a catalyst for change. It has transformed many things urban Indians are doing, rapidly. The way we discover fashion, buy clothes, toys, even the humble cauliflower, has changed dramatically. Can this modernisation in shopping habits be somehow linked to going 'green'? It's certainly a thought.

I like to believe that we have a head start over the West where conservation is concerned. We don't need to reinvent completely or think up new recycling models. The entire gamut of 'good and green' customer habits is already woven into the fabric of our society. They just need to be rekindled, protected against obsolescence and adapted to the way in which society is emerging.

For instance, can modern retail find a way of modernising

the traditional *raddiwala*, just as it did the fashion and grocery stores? It should not be too difficult. If customers are given easy and comfortable access to recycling outlets, they're going to adopt them within no time. Modern retail pioneer, Kishore Biyani, has been running an 'exchange mela' every March, on these lines. Even after 10 years and much dilution from the original simple idea, Big Bazaar's 'turn-in–your-old-stuff' campaign continues to have an appeal that is unmatched. How hard would it be for supermarkets and department stores to persuade customers to sell their old clothes, newspapers, CD players, CPU's, and make it look like the 'in' thing, thus turning it not just into a one-time marketing gimmick but a habit? Then again, can the delivery trucks that bring goods to the stores be used to carry back newspaper bundles, plastic waste, old clothes and other recyclable items to the warehouses on their return trips, thence to be shipped to recycling factories, at a profit?

Can retailers lead the way in making the use of jute and cloth shopping bags chic and a sign of modernity? Can they find a medium by which our customers can say 'no' to plastic without any major inconvenience to them?

If we put our minds to it, there are a host of such ideas waiting to be actualised. So while, for once, there is no readymade model from the West that can be copied, there is no need to. We must develop our own 'social technology' for conserving resources! Our heritage tells us that we can do so successfully.

MIND POKE

Every Indian woman has some broken, small or non-usable pieces of gold and silver jewellery tucked away into the drawer, often tied in an old handkerchief. I hope, someday a retailer of durables provides her with enough incentives to bring that out and help the family buy their next microwave or curved LED television! How is that for an idea!

Tell us on the Supermarketwala Facebook page. Please scan the QR Code using your smartphones to take you directly to the Facebook site.

PART 2

Retailing Habits

Elbow Push Factor

Any space more than an elbow length will always be breached or filled

RITU AGARWAL, A BANKER in Delhi, was on her way to London for an extended training trip. At the swanky new airport in Delhi, she stood in the check-in queue of the airline, and found something pushing against the back of her legs. When she looked back, she found the passenger behind her gesturing her to move forward, his baggage trolley nudging her ahead. Ritu found that there was a gap between her and the person in front, and the passenger behind her was urging her to close the gap. Ritu is a frequent international traveler because of her job, and nowhere is she prodded like this when she's in a queue. She moved ahead and all was well yet again. No more prodding.

Try this experiment anywhere in India—In a supermarket billing queue, keep a polite distance of about a foot and a half between your trolley and the shopper in front of you. Now count the number of ways in which fellow shoppers close the gap. See how someone simply comes along and steps right into the space in front. Just as you're sending the interloper to the back of the queue, you experience the slight but firm nudge on your lower calf from the trolley behind you. When you turn back, the person with the trolley will make a gentle gesture for you to move forward. If you continue to resist the myriad ways in which people try to force you into closing the gap, it will soon be used by people as a corridor for 'cutting' across to the other side.

Some time back, on my request, Piyul Mukherjee and her Proact consumer research team repeated this very curious experiment on queues of all kinds in urban India— at bus stops, train stations, airports, colleges, temples, fancy buffet counters in five star hotels, farmhouse marriage parties, and multiplexes. The findings were illuminating and near identical. The conclusion of the study read as follows:

'If you leave a space measuring more than your forearm— from the tip of your finger to your elbow—between you and the person just ahead of you in a queue, in India, such a gap is just not feasible to sustain. It shall get bridged or occupied within five minutes.'

We called this the 'Elbow Push Factor'.

It's interesting that the elbow push factor rule applies with equal validity across income and social strata. Most of us wouldn't agree. We've been brought up on Western notions of politeness and what constitutes civic behavior. We're outraged by such behavior. We are taught to give room, be patient and respect the personal space of a couple of feet around others. But the forearm rule tells us that our collective behavior is at complete variance with these notions of urban privacy. While we have 'learnt' to respect privacy, our inherent attitude towards it is somewhat different. For Indians, personal space isn't defined in physical terms. We see nothing wrong or disrespectful or invasive in jostling each other around. Intellectually we might find such behavior distasteful, but nonetheless it is part of our ethos and so cannot be dismissed. Quite simply, this is how we are.

But do designers of public spaces adequately take into account our 'need' for a little bit of crowding? That sounds funny. Are we really in need of crowding? How can anyone want to get crowded!?

The explanation isn't too difficult to find. Culturally, we have always had a bias towards the collective. Our instincts of family, community, chawl, and mohalla are still deep-rooted. Even our gods are not individual heroes, but 'family people', unlike in the west. In an overcrowded country like India, we are natural, instinctive, benign intruders into each others' lives. We see nothing wrong or uncouth in developing intimacy with another person, even a total stranger. We easily pick-up conversations with strangers while waiting for our flight to board, or to be served at a fast food restaurant, or even when we are sitting in a library. We are comfortable in crowded areas—weddings or marketplaces. So why should we balk at slight nudges in queues?

With crowding comes competition. For as long as we remember, we have had to compete for everything—for money, goods, space, and comfort. Need a bus? Push for a seat. Need college admission? Good luck with getting it! There are ten applicants jostling for each seat. Need to see your favourite god? Darshan queues at the temple can be twenty-four hours long. Less than a quarter of a century ago, you had to fight to get milk from a milk booth because of shortage. We have been competing with fellow shoppers, travelers, students, and devotees for getting just a little ahead.

In that mindset, 'wasting' precious queue space just does not gel with our instincts. A gap in the queue is a potential competitive risk that makes us uncomfortable.

Some western retail pundits talk about the 'butt-brush factor'. That is, people don't like getting jostled or bumped into, especially from behind. They get putoff and reduce or completely give up purchasing when they encounter the 'butt-brush factor' in a store. Ironically, in India, retailers who have taken this as gospel truth and worked hard to offer immunity from the butt-brush, find themselves struggling with inadequate numbers of customers. In the Indian scheme, luxurious and spacious layouts are decoded as wasteful and therefore expensive by average customers! Indeed the colloquial speak in Hindi for spacious stores is not 'shaant' (quiet or peaceful), but 'soona' (forlorn, empty).

In a nation of a billion aspirants and unparalleled population density, the shortage of space and its implications for our behavior are not going to vanish in a hurry. The queues with their 'elbow push factor' are here to stay for the foreseeable future. Those of us, who are space planners, educationists, temple trustees, marriage party hosts, or modern retailers, have to take this reality into account while designing our offerings. People actually feel reassured by a certain polite level of elbow push, a certain amount of crowding as long as it does not degenerate into disorder and chaos. Otherwise people feel disoriented and even disregarded. Keeping a vigil is as important as moving forward. And aren't we in a hurry to move forward?

MIND POKE

Is the whole notion of personal space v/s shared space, cultural and peculiar to some markets, or is it merely economic? As we get richer, more urban, will we grow out of the 'elbow push factor'? Let me know what you think.

Tell us on the Supermarketwala Facebook page. Please scan the QR Code using your smartphones to take you directly to the Facebook site.

Cheh Aankhen Baarah Haath!

A friends and family outing called shopping

'PREMAJI, HOW MANY TIMES have you visited a hypermarket, alone?'

'Never,' says Prema.

'And when do you shop at a neighbourhood grocery store alone?'

'Always, of course.'

Between these two questions lie huge implications for how the emerging modern retailers design their stores for the Indian market. If Prema always has someone with her when she goes to a supermarket, and is always alone when she goes to a neighbourhood store, it means that there is a difference in her attitude towards the two shopping formats. She has different expectations from each experience. She sees benefit in visiting a supermarket as part of a group instead of going alone. If we walk with Prema and count the *aankhen* (eyes) and *haath* (hands) that she has while she shops, we'll know where the difference lies. When Prema visits her neighbourhood grocer, she has '*do aankhen*' and '*do haath*'. But this isn't the case when she visits the supermarket. Let's see how.

This is a typical supermarket visit for Prema. Kailash, her husband, drives Prema and their daughter Vinita, a bubbly 10 year old, in their new WagonR, for their monthly shopping trip to the new modern bazaar in their upcoming neighbourhood in Ahmedabad. Prema carries a shopping list, since she knows Kailash might become impatient, and she cannot afford to forget any of her 'must buy' items for the month. Vinita is always the first one to run into the store and pull out a trolley. It always starts with the supermarket section of the store, with Prema picking up her usual toiletries and things for the home. Vinita is always attracted by the biscuits and snacks sections. Though only ten, she is smart enough to pick out the best offer on her favorite chocolate biscuits and get her mummy to add them to the trolley. She knows what the offer signs look like, and freely moving in the aisle gives her an opportunity to browse around. It is a delight to feast one's eyes on so many varieties of biscuits, and pick up the packets of one's choice. Sometimes her mother forces her to discard something that she has put in the trolley, and they stand there and argue over the decision before finally arriving at a truce. In these shopping trips to the supermarket, Vinita is very much a part of the decision-making process.

A little later, the trolley is transferred into Kailash's charge, who is happy to play the 'gatherer' of the goodies that the mother and daughter duo hunt from the jungle of shelves and bins. He is only partially involved in their 'search and grab' sallies, but as he follows them down the various aisles, he too keeps an eye cocked for new products and offers. This Saturday, a manufacturer of tea has put up a tasting stall in the tea aisle. It isn't a brand they are familiar with. Kailash tastes the tea and puts one box in the trolley, his personal contribution to the household shopping. Prema heads to the rice counter, and soon has some doubt about the difference in price between two varieties of rice. She calls upon Kailash and they mutually decide on which one is of better quality. Prema discovers that her favourite Kashmiri chillies are missing from the aisle. Again Kailash comes to her aid by sending the store assistant to look for the chillies.

There is a distinct difference in the manner in which Prema behaves when shopping in a neighbourhood, traditional store versus when she visits a modern supermarket. There is a reason why she goes to the supermarket with her family, and it's not convenience. When Prema was the sole shopper for her family, she was picking up signs and signals around her with her own senses, but now there is an interesting multiplier at play when the family shops as a threesome. The extra pairs of eyes, hands, and ears are attuned to different stimuli, driven by their own interests, needs, wants, and temptations. Prema doesn't have the same approach to biscuits as Vinita, and isn't as easily persuaded to buy a new brand of tea as Kailash. While Prema picks things that are familiar and tested, Kailash and Vinita are less fettered by habit and more inclined to explore and pick up new things, new deals. They are more excitable and eager to browse in the aisles. They can pick up on new stimuli much faster than Prema, who is bound by habit, thus seeing only what she knows and ignoring the rest. In the last trip, for instance, Kailash noticed a large banner, displayed in another section, promoting an offer on a non-stick pan. He remembered Prema saying that they could do with a new pan. Kailash decided to step across the aisle to the home goods section and check out the offer. In the end Kailash's small distraction resulted in them buying the pan.

Prema and Kailash's shopping behaviour is reflected across thousands of Indian families who are getting used to the modern way of shopping. The family, or sometimes friends and even neighbours, shop as a unit. Every member of the family participates in the decision-making process. Each person has the power to 'hunt' for things, and thus the collective becomes the shopping unit, not the individual. The shopping trolley is a reflection of the tastes and preferences of the entire family, and is the result of a group effort. The members of the group depend more on each other rather than the store assistants. They are not confused by the plethora of messages and inputs coming at them within the store. Rather they revel in them. The messages address different people at different times. While Prema might ignore what's going on in the shaving products aisle, Kailash won't. This is even truer for impulse purchases. Kailash and Vinita both provide the extra 'eyes' that are so loved by marketers.

In a traditional store, there is no flexibility offered to the shopper. She has to be dependent on the store assistant, whether she likes it or not. Her shopping basket reflects her own needs and the shop assistant's recommendations. There's no room for any other input. Prema has '*do aankhen, do haath*' where her household shopping is concerned.

From the foregoing we can see that with the advent of modern retail, the Premas in India are no longer in the '*do aankhen, do haath*' mode. Instead they have been transformed into '*cheh aankhen, baarah haath*' and beyond, as they come to the stores equipped with myriad senses, multiple temperaments, multiple needs and wants, all shopping together.

Contrast this with what happens in the West, where both the society and stores are better geared for the individual than the group. Prema's counterpart in Toronto, Brenda, invariably shops alone, literally in the '*do aankhen, do haath*' manner. Even though she is married, grocery shopping is almost never a family experience. Brenda is seldom excited by the offers that supermarkets in her town bring to her. In their home, going to the supermarket is a chore, not part of their monthly entertainment. Sure enough, the designs of stores that serve Prema and Brenda can't possibly be the same.

Stores like the modern bazaar in Prema's locality that throw lots of stimuli, even if distracting, at the shopper are likely to benefit from one of Prema's 'extra' senses picking them up and thus leading to a sale. Anyone who shops with kids knows the impact of such 'distractions' on the shopping basket too well. Prema's shopping experience is rounded off by the assistance lent to her by all the people who help her with her purchases right up to the point of use, the store assistant who pushes her full trolley to their car, the security staff in their building who helps with the bags and even the maid who helps in storing everything properly once it is bought. Prema's '*do haath*' are in effect '*baarah haath*'!

The introduction of multiple variants, new products, more of everything is a very recent phenomenon. It is exciting to walk down the store aisles and feast one's eyes on the sheer variety of goods, a big change from times past when a soap came in three brands and two sizes. In this phase of shopping evolution, the aspiring class in India is enjoying the new celebration of choice and discovery. Shopping for the daily needs of life is still far from being a humdrum chore to be quickly dispensed with, like it is for Brenda. The shared responsibility of choices and indulgences also means family bonding and fun. The shopping multiplier of '*cheh aankhen baarah haath*' is here to stay. Retailers who understand this and build their stores to service the aspiring and excitable customers will be rewarded. In contrast, retailers who launch small, narrow range, sanitized stores to help customers 'finish the chore of shopping' quickly, are likely to miss a trick in the great Indian celebration of consumption creation.

MIND POKE

Next time at a clothing store spot a woman shopping with a woman companion and another woman shopper, with a male companion. What are the behavioral differences that you can spot?

Tell us on the Supermarketwala Facebook page. Please scan the QR Code using your smartphones to take you directly to the Facebook site.

Copy Shopping or Social Proofing

In the hunt for grabbing the best deals, copy shopping comes handy

ANJU SAXENA FINDS THE hypermarket in her neighbourhood in Malad in Mumbai, slightly overwhelming. It is so huge. And it is spread over three levels, with the first level devoted only to groceries, the second only to apparel and the third only to home goods and electronics. Most of the time, Anju visits only the ground floor. A few weeks ago, Anju spotted a pair of pillows in another shopper's trolley at the check-out. The pillows were taped together, and Anju guessed that there was some kind of deal being offered on those pillows. She asked her daughter to guard her trolley while she made a quick trip to the second floor, to the pillow and mattress section. There was, indeed, a deal on the foam pillows and since Anju had been thinking of replacing a couple of her old pillows, she was quick to grab the deal. Anju confessed that had it not been for the act of peeping into a fellow-shopper's trolley, she would never have availed the offer on her own. The store, of course, benefited from this phenomenon, now popularly referred to in the retail world as 'copy shopping'.

Anju never thought she would be proud of her copying skills, until she went to buy a sari and picked up one from another shopper's potential selections. The kurta that she wears and is universally liked by her friends and family,wasn't picked up from a catalogue, but from a design that Anju saw another woman wearing at the tailor's shop.

In the good old days, before the advent of self-service stores, shoppers relied on an expert to help them take decisions, to get the best deals, in order to follow the latest fashion trends. This was the quintessential neighbourhood shopkeeper. The advice might not have been one hundred percent reliable, but where it lost on believability, it won hands-down on the reassurance factor. How often have we heard our trusty shopkeeper say, 'Aaj kal yehi chalta hai?' And therefore taken his advice, without any hesitation?

There's no such person at the modern retail stores to say that to us, who's advice would be words etched in stone, advice that you would follow without a second thought. When we shop, we are on our own, except for the messages flung at us by the hundreds of notices hanging from all the racks, announcing and telling us about the various deals. The information is there, but what about the reassurance? Where is the stand-in for the man behind the counter who knows it all? Who will tell us 'aaj kal kya chalta hai.'? This phenomenon is called the 'social proof' by consumer-behaviour pundits. That there are other people buying a product, reduces the risk of choice felt by the customer. Both, the new age self-service and web-based retailers have to find new tricks to bring alive the good old social proof assurance of the bazaar days.

Anju has evolved a method to understand what the general trend is. She goes around the aisles of the hypermarket to find the best deals, but also keeps an eye firmly on the other trolleys that wheel around her to discover some trend or deal that she might have missed out on.

Smart store managers have also evolved substitutes for the friendly neighbourhood 'advisor'. A simple idea that a manager in a store at Thane has adopted is a 'trend' trolley, a trolley that contains the best offers in the store. The trolley is taken around the floor. And that's all! There are some e-commerce sites that run a ticker at the bottom of the web page that keeps showing pictures of items 'just ordered'. There need to be many such new tricks to reassure us that other people are already buying what we are hesitating to decide about! It helps.

Copy shopping is particularly in evidence when it comes to fashion trends. What is one of the biggest influences on a woman's choice of what she wears? It isn't advertisements or fashion articles. It is what the neighbour, friend, fellow-shopper is wearing. At marriages, often women change in a common area, and exchange notes on the latest trends in saris, jewellery, shoes, and handbags. At parties and other celebrations, women naturally observe the minute details of other guests' apparel, and mental notes are taken on what one's next purchase should be. It isn't fashion editors who choose for us what our sleeve's pattern should be, but the woman next door.

And so, at apparel stores, the most happening place is the fitting room area. Women keep an eye out for what the others are trying out, and more often than not, get ideas on patterns, colours, embellishments by looking at what the other person is wearing. The voiceless exchange of ideas is more potent than any picture of a model on the wall. Instinctively, the female community of shoppers recognises this, and encourages its members to freely offer and seek advice. Oftentimes the word of a stranger is what creates the turning point in a decision. At a Primark outlet in Oxford Street, London, I saw precisely this phenomenon. It was 'Sale' time and women were changing tops in a corner of the women's section. The by-product of this communal behaviour was their eagerness to help each other with suggestions.

It is company policy to keep a rack of outfits outside the fitting rooms at some global apparel chains. These outfits are picked up from the fitting rooms after the shoppers have left and hung there for other shoppers to make a note of. At a single place, the shopper can see for herself what her fellow-shoppers are going for. The silent suggestion is powerful in the way it is positioned. An even more potent, but drastic alternative could be to offer the customers a choice of a communal trial room, in addition to the existing partitioned, personal trial rooms. In the shared trial rooms, multiple shoppers could try out their tops and kurta's, etc. Shoppers coming alone will benefit from the plethora of advice that they will receive from others in that trial room. They will see what others are wearing, and need not make any effort to figure trends for themselves. And of course, the noise and cheer of a communal location is always an uplifting experience, as wedding guests will testify to.

While modern shopping formats have eliminated the friendly but slightly intrusive shopkeeper, there are ways to manage the shopper's need to pick information from other fellow shoppers—directly or tacitly. Such information builds reassurance and increases sales. Isn't social media chatter about a brand or store also a strong social proofing factor? To my mind, the impact of your product sitting gloriously in a fellow customer's trolley and the presence of your brand in a friend's Facebook post is worth more than many columns of print advertising, for sure.

MIND POKE

E-Commerce is where shoppers are the loneliest. Visit Hotels.com and see the number of smart ways in which they make you feel, you are not alone. Have you come across any such new, innovative uses of social proofing?

Tell us on the Supermarketwala Facebook page. Please scan the QR Code using your smartphones to take you directly to the Facebook site.

in mind, the impact of your product while obviously in a fellow customer's trolley and the presence of your brand in friends' Facebook post is worth more than many columns of print advertising, for sure.

MIND POST

E-Commerce is large shoppers are the [illegible]. Visit Flipkart.com and see the number of smart ways in which they make consumers purchase not alone through connections, but such new [illegible] the rise of social proofing.

Follow us on the Supermarket Facebook page. Please scan the QR Code using your smartphones to take you directly to the Facebook page.

Servicing Lifetime Value

IT WAS A SUNDAY EVENING at a renowned department store in town.

'Sir, the alteration desk is on the third floor. Go right from the elevator. Towards the end of the floor, under the staircase, next to the washrooms,' said the polite cashier, as she billed a pair of trousers and a jacket I had just bought. Up the elevator, at the end of the hall, with help from another friendly floor staff, I found the alteration desk. They accepted the trousers I had just bought, which needed a small length reduction.

'You can collect your trousers anytime between 4 and 7 pm on weekdays,' said the attendant while handing me a slip of paper.

'What?' I exclaimed. 'It's just a ten minute job. I'll just walk around in the store or maybe have a coffee at the food court and come by to pick them up,' I offered.

'No sir. The tailor comes only in the morning and we do not deliver alterations when the store is busy in the evenings and on weekends.'

I felt bewildered and tried to work out in my head the complex project of picking up my trousers. I live 3 kms away and on weekdays, work 25 kms away at the other end of town.

I was going to have to make another trip for my trousers, for which I had paid top dollar just a few minutes back!

I walked out of the store thinking that just a few minutes ago when I was selecting a jacket and a pair of trousers in the men's section, I was made to feel welcome. The staff offered me a cold drink and a competent attendant helped me go through choices and even offered style advice. I was a very important person for the store and they knew a thing or two about making me feel that way. What perplexed me was when I had paid up, the same store offered me the rough end of the rule book and they wanted to deal with me only during lean hours on weekdays when they were not 'busy' with paying customers!

The situation is not so dire in most stores, but the fundamental instinct remains—a paying customer is more important than a non-paying one. As a matter of fact, they are both the same person. The difference is in the transaction, not the individual. The transaction changes, that's all.

As a retailer of products or services, here is a revealing exercise to do. Get a pencil, a sheet of paper, and a calculator.

1. How much approximately does a customer spend, every time she is in your store? (average bill value) Rs________
2. How many times do you think a normal, loyal customer shops with you in a year? (frequency of purchase) ______times
3. What's the average margin you make in your store? (gross margin percentage) ________%

4. For how many years, roughly, is a regular customer likely to shop with you? ______years

When we multiply the values in 1, 2, 3, and 4, we get the total gross profit our business stands to make, from the customer. This is called her lifetime value. The lifetime value of the average customer for your business is, let's assume Rs 30,000. If you wish to be more accurate you can discount gross profit of each subsequent year by, say, 10 percent, to get a more accurate net present value. For a supermarket, this value is about Rs 25,000.

Here's the revealing next question that makes many things clear about our service policies, especially post-purchase service and grievance handling—When the customer returns a product for replacement, asks for alteration or has any dispute with the store, what's the value/cost involved, in the transaction?

In the grocery business the value is Rs 50. I have done this lifetime value v/s average dispute value comparison across grocers, department stores, gyms, beauty salons, fast food places, and even consulting firms. The conclusion is the same no-brainer. It is not wise to take even the smallest risk with the lifetime value of a customer, over the average dispute value.

More often than not, store teams can be found telling the customers, 'But you do not have a receipt; you have already used 25 percent of the rice/biscuit/cereal that you are unhappy with and returning.' From their viewpoint, the customer service desk people are handling a Rs 50 transaction and protecting their company's interest. But the business stands to risk losing Rs 25,000 worth of custom.

So which way would you as a retailer want the dispute settled? The answer is obvious, yet so very often, we find the principle missing in practice.

The reason, in my view, is that the customer service desk, alteration desks, goods-return counters are 'cost' items in most retail set-ups. Revenues are made at the cash tills and other places are costs, to be controlled and minimised. Instead, if these are seen as customer lifetime value protectors, many a behaviour will easily alter.

Famous global consultants, McKinsey, have built into their service delivery the awareness of lifetime value of the client. Often, on their first assignment with a large client, they over-deliver output to such an extent that at a project level, the effort put on that assignment is far too costly for McKinsey. But it delights the client and keeps them interested in the consultants for a long time. They advise big businesses around the world on retaining customers. It is not surprising they take this approach, since they practice what they preach!

Almost all customers are decent people. I would look at any grievance or service demand they make as an opportunity to delight them. How we handle their request may keep them interested in our store for a long time. It is smart to keep our teams thinking these are good people, instead of being sharp about catching the odd customer misusing our liberal service policies. I would never risk Rs 25,000 of profit for a Rs 20-pack of cream biscuits gone wrong, would you? So let's just smile, say sorry and replace it—fast! No questions asked!

MIND POKE

Entrepreneur retailers are very good at delivering a delight on 'returns policy'. Check it out at your Kirana shop or your fruit seller. They intuitively know your 'lifetime value' and act on it, in real time—something the organized stores can never match! What do you say!

Tell us on the Supermarketwala Facebook page. Please scan the QR Code using your smartphones to take you directly to the Facebook site.

Touch Me, Talk to Me

SWATI DESAI BELONGS TO a well-to-do household in Ahmedabad and does all her shopping at a large supermarket. Until recently Swati was used to shopping at the local store, but the new supermarket had so many attractive offers that Swati quickly moved most of her shopping to it. It was a very different shopping experience, where everything was arranged on shelves and Swati found she could reach out and pick up anything she liked. Until the day she was so tempted by a new shampoo that she couldn't resist flipping open its top to see how it smelt. She almost poured a little into her palm to feel its texture before she realized that what she was doing was probably 'illegal' and looked around furtively! Was she allowed to assess the shampoo in this manner? She was not sure, so she put the shampoo back and moved on quickly, resisting looking back over her shoulder.

It is a known fact that the human experience uses all five senses of sight, hearing, taste, touch, and smell, if not simultaneously then at least two senses at a time. Shopkeepers in India have known this fact instinctively and used it to sell their wares over the centuries. When you visit the local mithaiwala, he will offer you samples of the sweets for tasting. Who can resist buying after the taste experience?

At a Baskin Robbins outlet, does one ever reject purchasing, after the delightful mouthfuls in those tiny spoons that are on offer for tasting? The aroma of freshly baked bread or freshly ground coffee is so irresistible that one is almost lured into buying these things against one's wish. Even a child cannot resist passing her fingers through a heap of grain that is on offer in sacks in most kirana shops. The very act of touching the grain and feeling it slide through one's fingers is enough reassurance to the diligent housewife that she is buying the right stuff. She is least bothered that multiple hands have also 'caressed' the same grain all through the time it lies there in the open. Shopkeepers, both traditional and modern, seem to know instinctively how to engage multiple senses at the time of purchase.

Now look at the practice for most leading product brands. Swati Desai doesn't have the option of trying out any of the products that she was offered in the supermarket. She has no choice but to rely on the marketers' claims that she has seen on primetime television, about the special features of the products, their exotic new perfume, taste, even multi-hued look complete with streaks in soaps, for instance, since all these are usually sealed in opaque packaging. Before modern retail hit the Indian landscape, the marketers' hesitation in giving direct access to FMCG products to the customer was understandable. Conventional shops did not have the kind of environment where product experience could be facilitated. It was like meeting your date at a crowded bus stop. There's only so much one can do to get closer to the other person. Perhaps one can shake hands and smile. Even holding hands is not permitted. The interaction is formal and there is no opportunity for intimacy. One is forced to keep one's distance. And so, marketers relied only on bright, loud packaging to attract attention. Now compare meeting at a bus stop to dating in a restaurant. The possibilities in this new situation are unlimited. Tantalizing. One can talk, hold hands, relax, let go of the stiffness. Modern retail is your brand's date with the consumer in a restaurant. The opportunity and environment for getting close and personal with the customer is far greater than in a conventional store. The product can literally speak to the customer in a one-on-one interaction. It can reveal itself to the customer, and offer her a greater opportunity to decide on its merits, something that is denied to her today.

Multi-sensorial marketing is yet to come of age in India, perhaps because marketers do not recognize the scope of the opportunity that modern retail offers to them. Unknown to perhaps the customer herself, today she continues to choose based on the old ways of merely looking at products. But doing things differently does seem to matter. A very large brand of soap, for example, is lagging behind in the new shower gel category, while a small player has raced ahead. The latter has transparent packaging and the gel is also transparent while the former is completely opaque. The visual stimulus that the latter offers is certainly more powerful. Now imagine if there was a sample dispenser on the shelf that said 'Try me', what would be the effect on the consumer? Firstly, she would certainly feel welcome to try it. The mere act of opening the flip top, smelling the contents, maybe even squirting some on her palm, would 'speak' to her in ways that advertising never can do. A transparent tube of toothpaste, with the gleaming crystals sparkling through the gel, persuades the consumer that this toothpaste is special, no matter how the other gels are promoted. There is something sensually exciting about feeling the product.

In conventional kirana shops, the products were always stacked out of reach of the customer, and she had to depend on the shopkeeper to hand over the things to her. There was hardly any opportunity to interact with the product. It was a rather cold transaction, and her real interaction with the packs only began at home. The first thing modern retail has done, as we saw in an earlier chapter 'Shopkeeper-in-Law', is to remove the 'shopkeeper – a man' from the transaction. The customer now selects things for herself, and it is for marketers to work out more and more ways of pushing their products off the shelves and into the shopper's hands.

Why can't juices be tasted? Why can't moisturizing lotions be touched? Why can't new foods be offered for tasting? Why can't soaps be packaged differently so that they can be seen?

It's well-known that Swati Desai and her sister—shoppers all over the world—spend just a fraction of a minute 'looking' at a brand on the shelf. You get a tenfold increase in her attention if you invite her to 'touch, smell, see, taste or try' your brand. Wars have been fought through centuries for gaining a woman's attention. Brand owners now have a new battle on their hands that they need to win, for this very attention.

MIND POKE

Try and visit some supermarkets and locate examples of packs designed for energizing customers, in a self-service environment.

Tell us on the Supermarketwala Facebook page. Please scan the QR Code using your smartphones to take you directly to the Facebook site.

Habit-Buying or Frequent Swayamvar?

PIYUL GUPTA'S APARTMENT IN Powai, a suburb in Mumbai, has two bathrooms. Both bathrooms contain multiple shower gels, two different face wash brands, three different brands of soap, and two different brands of toothpaste.

'We normally buy the same brands from the supermarket,' Piyul asserts. 'Sometimes when Isha (Piyul's ten year old daughter) is with me, she picks up new things for herself and us.' The bathroom shelf clearly contradicted this testimony. So how did this happen?

In our annual 'pantry audit' surveys of consumer homes and subsequent chats with homemakers, we discovered that when they say 'same brand' they actually mean 'similar brands'. So if this month a homemaker has bought a particular brand of shower gel and body lotion, there is every likelihood of her buying something different next month. Within her 'consideration set' she plays 'kabhi Nivea, kabhi Vaseline' without fuss, and often without realising it! As long as it's within the same category, Piyul and many others like her pick up what appeals to them at that time.

It was not always like this with Piyul. This is a change from her past behaviour, and has happened quite recently. It is not a coincidence that it happened when she started frequenting a supermarket. In the past, when she patronised the local grocer, she invariably asked to buy a particular brand and pack size, for instance, 'Bada Pantene'. She articulated her brand preference clearly and unambiguously.

Perhaps that's the behaviour that marketers of the current era have grown up studying. The conventional wisdom offered by text books is that, '70 percent of consumer products choices are made out of sheer habit. You largely buy what you bought last time.'

But Piyul, a conventional customer, defies that paradigm. Unknowingly, she plays between brands in the same category, exchanging Pantene for Clinic, and Pepsodent for Colgate almost all the time. It was high time this new behaviour was investigated. So we set out to do a status check, by asking aspiring urban folks two questions—How many soap, shower gel, hand wash, face wash, shampoo, and body lotion brands do you have on your bathroom shelf right now? Last month, how many of them were different?

The answers were, to say the least, a revelation and pose fresh challenges to conventional marketing thinking.

Piyul didn't switch brands before the advent of the modern retail era. To switch brands in the pre-modern retail era had to be necessarily a pre-determined decision, one that was reached at much before entering the store. You went to the store, asked for what you wanted and got out of there quickly. You also could not appear confused and indecisive in front of the knowledgeable shopkeeper, or seek his help in browsing through brands, firstly because he had no time for the interaction, and also because you knew that he did not possess an in-depth knowledge of the product he was selling. Therefore, in a conventional grocery store, one merely executed one's ready-to-buy shopping list.

Consider Piyul's behaviour now inside the supermarket . She is free to approach the shampoo aisle, easy and undecided, check all the options and pick whichever brand that appeals to her the most without having to bother about the wiser-than-thou kirana store owner. One could almost think of Piyul's curiosity and indecisiveness as a kind of 'flirting'. She merely looks at her 'usual' brand without committing herself. She browses through the entire rack, examines the choices that fall within her consideration set and then picks up whatever meets her fancy at that moment. Sometimes it's the same brand as the last time, more often it is not. For instance if Nivea Body Lotion is offering a discount, then she'll probably choose it over Dove. Sometimes it's only curiosity at play. A new brand or a new variant attracts attention, and Piyul confesses to getting persuaded in trying it out.

Infact, if brands were folks and we had relationships with them, then the earlier method of buying from the neighbourhood store was more like a 'marriage', where month-in-month-out we bought the same brands, simply for a lack of any other options or way of exercising it, or just as a matter of habit. Honestly speaking, brand preferences were habits, more than anything else. At the time of selection, there may have been a hint of preference, but over a period of time, one bought what one did merely because one didn't see a convenient way of changing it.

Contrast this with the new marketplace. If shopping in the conventional retail format can be likened to marriage, then in the new marketplace, the relationship paradigm has visibly changed to one of 'dating and mating' with like-minded brands. One enters the store with a basic set of requirements, and then one picks up whatever suits these the most!

Every time Piyul walks down the supermarket aisle, it's a fresh round of 'swayamwar', where brands have to be well turned out, wear their most attractive sparkles and trinkets in order to catch her attention. Clearly, that she asked you out last time and even liked being with you, does not automatically make you the 'chosen one' next time around. Your competitor may wear a smarter outfit or have a better party line, next time. After all, anything is possible when a relationship has no strings attached!

If the shop shelves are where the monthly 'swayamwar' is to be held, individual brands will have to fight to look their best and work with the store ownership to be first-in-line for the customer's attention. Another important aspect—in the 'dating and mating' way of conducting relationships amongst people, a whole array of services are built up. Party venues, restaurants, multiplexes, lounge clubs, all these are required far more as courtship places than if people 'settled down' quickly with a partner.

In the same manner, brand 'swayamvars' need an important service—supermarkets. Without these 'courtship venues' there would be no avenues for the aspiring new brands. In fact, the two things feed-off each other. More supermarkets mean more brand 'dating and mating', which in turn need more supermarkets.

As people get financially better off, they aspire more, consume more, they use product brands as a ladder to climb up the lifestyle wall and lead better lives. They enjoy the feeling of choice, and flirting with multiple brands, not just in stores, but even at home. With multiple brands in her bathroom shelf, Piyul switches from one to another 'in shower' so to speak, foregoing loyalty in favour of choice. The look of an array of products on her bathroom shelf also gives her a moment of satisfaction.

Clearly, in the new era of modern retail, the conventional wisdom of repurchase doesn't hold water. In the new reality, especially when it comes to simpler items like soaps, shower gels and body lotions, the customer is more than happy to swtich from one brand to the other, at times using all of them simultaneously. Brands will have to recognise this changed paradigm and find new ways of accompanying the customer on her way to the shower, every month. There is no point in bemoaning the absence of the good old days of brand loyalty. Marketers must recognise the new lens through which their product is perceived, and innovate accordingly. We live in interesting times, with both modern and conventional retail existing side by side. However, while retail is crossing the divide slowly, marketers must decide which side of the fence they're going to sit on, follow the age-old textbook method, or create a new vocabulary for the flirtatious customer.

MIND POKE

So, how many brands of bathing soaps and bodywash gels do you stock at home? Do you also stock as many brands of body lotions and breakfast cereals? How loyal are you to a particular brand? My view—households that go shopping at the supermarkets, brand loyalty is clearly one notch lower than in regular kirana shopping homes. True? Our last kitchen audit showed on average 1.9 breakfast cereals per home, oats excluded! What do you have to say?

Tell us on the Supermarketwala Facebook page. Please scan the QR Code using your smartphones to take you directly to the Facebook site.

Look Familiar, Feel Familiar, and I'll be Friends

RASHMI GUPTA IS THIRTY six years old, and has been married for thirteen years. She works in a bank, while her husband is a marketing executive with a pharmaceutical company. They live in the western suburb of Goregaon in Mumbai. With a full-time job, Rashmi barely has any time for her shopping. The mall that opened in the neighbourhood six years ago has been the biggest improvement in Rashmi's life in this period. Rashmi hasn't entirely forgotten her old life of shopping on the go, of picking up fresh produce from vendors who sit with baskets near the suburban train station, of the return journey home being a 'treasure hunt' of groceries, the eye alertly scouting for relevant purchases while her mind was too tired to think. Sometimes, Rashmi recalls, she would have to let go of her preciously acquired auto mid-journey as she remembered something she needed to pick up for that evening's dinner. Shopping was always an ordeal, an unnecessary interruption in some well-deserved rest.

The mall and the attendant supermarket changed all that. With everything under one roof, all Rashmi needed to do was make a list of groceries—buying supplies for home was now a mere half hour job during the weekend. More often than not, the trip for groceries is combined with a family outing, dinner, and a movie in the mall multiplex. The supermarket is well-stocked and the fresh produce section has everything in neatly ordered rows. The fresh vegetables are kept in bins in the middle of the section, and the exotic and chopped vegetables as well as some greens line the chillers along the sides. Everything is well-lit, and everything is in the same place every time Rashmi visits. There are no surprises and Rashmi's tired mind likes that.

In the meat and fish section also, Rashmi is vastly relieved by the reprieve from going to smelly markets. Here, in the supermarket, everything is kept in neat rows in very sanitized surroundings. The workers, in their aprons and gloves, look hygienic. Rashmi cannot check for the freshness of the fish by examining its eye, but she trusts the store to stock the best quality produce. Again, in this section as well, everything is predictable. There's no need to ask the shop assistant if a certain product is in stock on that day. The store doesn't follow too much seasonal variation in stocking.

One day, Rashmi's bank was closed and she decided to step out to complete some errands. While walking to her destination, she encountered a vegetable cart piled high with carrots, this being carrot season. The carrots looked fresh and enticing and Rashmi, on an impulse, bought a couple of kilos, justifying the purchase on the grounds of cost, though in her mind she knew that there wasn't much difference between the prices here and inside the supermarket. It was the lure of the cart, overflowing with carrots that had attracted Rashmi.

Before the advent of the supermarket, Rashmi used to make an occasional visit to the vegetable market in the neighbouring suburb of Malad. Once every couple of months or so, she would take an armload of shopping bags and wade through the heaps of vegetables strung around through those narrow lanes. At a glance, Rashmi could spot the seasonal vegetables. They would always be prominently displayed all through the market. In spite of the piled-up garbage everywhere, and the overall look of civic degradation, there was something cheerful about the market. The sight of so much produce provided a sort of reassurance that the customer was getting the choicest fruits and vegetables at a reasonable price, that it was okay to buy more and celebrate the sight of plenitude. The same went for fish. The fish market with its unbearable squalor and stink, yet offers a tempting array of fresh catch and there's an element of seasonality in the kinds of fish that are given prominence from month to month.

One certainly doesn't get this feeling in a modern store. The template for display is standard all year round, and in this sanitized world one almost feels insulated from reality. There is very little to indicate if it's apple season, or carrot season, or even mango season. Were it not for the fact, for example, that mangoes are available only for three months in the year, and therefore their presence in the store signifies seasonality, the customer would not find anything distinct in the display in the normal course. Things that are available all through the year have lost their place in store displays. They have no identity of their own and no significance either. Winter, for instance, is the season for celebrating greens. One wouldn't know it just from looking at a modern store. Greens are kept on a separate shelf, and stay in the very same place all year round. The lure of traditional markets lies in countering this anesthetizing effect of shelf space allocation.

The Indian supermarket model has been, for the most part, borrowed from the West. There isn't much difference between store displays here and there. Fresh produce is kept in a similar mix of refrigerated and unrefrigerated environments. Over a period of time, Western shopping habits have become accustomed to the absence of wet markets. A number of factors have restricted the presence of wet markets, especially in the developed world. Customers have no choice but to buy from supermarkets, and have limited exposure to vegetable and fish markets. Interestingly enough, where access is provided, customers embrace these wholeheartedly. Witness the popularity of farmers markets, as and when they spring up. There is a feeling that the produce here is fresher, having travelled less than the antiseptic vegetables in a chain grocery store.

In India, traditional and wet markets are going to continue to hold their own against modern retail for the foreseeable future. So why should there be such a stark difference between modern and traditional retail? In a bid to create change, retailers seem to have discarded many practices that connect Indians to their cultural roots. It is a fact that nuclear families are only now becoming more widespread in urban India. Many families still have 'a connect' with their 'native place', and often, traditional markets are one way of building a bridge to the family's roots back home. Many families, for instance, still buy their spices in the spring when they are freshest, and preserve them for the entire year. Peas are often shelled and frozen for consumption through the year. During mango season, advantage is taken of the availability and price to extract mango pulp and freeze it. The consumption of fish during the winter months automatically rises, not that one would know it from seeing the meat and fish section of the supermarket.

One of the ways modern retail can win the hearts of customers is to bring in a touch of tradition into the store. It isn't difficult to create the feeling of the marketplace inside the store. It requires imagination more than any other resource. And the multiplier effect this will have on customer loyalty will be huge. An early hypermarket called Giant in Hyderabad decided to celebrate a 'rice festival' in the month of January when the new crop becomes available. The store saw its word-of-mouth marketing go up significantly. It became associated not just with rice but the overall availability of *all* foodgrains. And all because for a month, the store set-up an aesthetically designed display of different varieties of rice and chose to stock 25 kilo bags, so that customers got the feeling that they were buying what they would in a wholesale market. The interesting thing is that after a couple of years, the store stopped the display for reasons of space and logistics, but by now it didn't need to. Its reputation as a supplier of quality foodgrain was now firmly entrenched.

There are unlimited possibilities for a model that combines the orderliness of modern retail with the marketplace feel of traditional stores. A point to be noted is that while modern retail can adopt something from traditional markets, the reverse isn't true! In this equation, therefore, modern retail will definitely be a winner.

In India, customers still revel in the presence of tradition. Festivals, rituals, foods, nothing has disappeared, only adapted to modern living. If modern retail accepts this reality and adapts to it, its acceptability and popularity will grow manifold.

MIND POKE

Which supermarket or department store in you town is most connected with the community? Send us a picture and a few lines about it.

Tell us on the Supermarketwala Facebook page. Please scan the QR Code using your smartphones to take you directly to the Facebook site.

PART 3

Crunch Time

Thanda Matlab... *Baasi!*

'COME QUICKLY, THE FOOD will get cold,' is Prerna's normal call to the family every evening when she serves dinner. She doesn't like delays, even small ones, in consuming the food, as with each extra minute that her husband and her ten year old daughter take to come to the dinner table, the food grows cold, and, according to Prerna, less tasty. Prerna always serves freshly-cooked, hot food when the family eats together. In her opinion, it is bad enough that her husband has to eat a packed lunch on weekdays. She sees no reason why the family shouldn't eat hot, freshly cooked food for dinner. Like all Indian parents, Prerna and her husband like to finish everything on their plate and persuade their daughter, Rhea, to do the same. Prerna is happy when she serves out the last spoon of *dal* from the serving bowl. Making just the right quantity of *dal* or curry, that gets 'finished' at the dining table, is a minor triumph. Refrigerating leftovers is not a part of our culture. Prerna is a homemaker, and keeps aside a part of the evening for cooking dinner. She takes pride in serving up authentic food that has not come out of any packet.

One peep into Prerna's refrigerator—the freezer section

has in neatly stacked rows an assortment of dry *masalas*, grated coconut, ginger-garlic paste, packets of milk, frozen peas, and corn. In the refrigerator section, she has fresh vegetables, eggs, butter, yogurt, bottles of jam, ketchup, a loaf of bread, some chocolate, and a little dough. There is little cooked food kept in the fridge. A little bit of curry that no one wanted to 'finish' and some *dal*. Prerna is always uncomfortable with leftovers, and usually gives them away to her maid. She always likes to serve food that has just been cooked. Leftovers are somehow not considered a healthy practice. Perhaps this is to do with the tropical Indian climate, where the heat spoils food faster. Even with state-of-the-art refrigeration, one is never completely sure if the food hasn't spoiled or so many people believe.

In faraway New Jersey, recent migrants Swapna and Abhishek lead very busy lives, with both of them working. Swapna spends most of her Sunday cooking four types of vegetables, a *dal* and some pulav, and freezes them separately, one for each day of the week. During the week, there's no time to cook, and Abhishek only has to microwave that day's dish and serve. With people like them, such behaviour is normal. Almost everyone they know does the same thing, although each time the couple entertains its Indian friends, they make it a point to serve freshly cooked food. Sundays, for Swapna and Abhishek, are special because they get to eat fresh Indian food, a real treat. The point to be noted is that when they were in India, neither of them considered the option of reheating and consuming meals cooked in advance although both of them had almost the same schedule here as well.

Indians are wired to believe that food is best eaten fresh. Women are reluctant to have a gap between cooking and serving / eating food. The belief is that freshly cooked food is healthy and tasty. It is a way of showing one's care, love and concern for the person for whom the food is cooked and served. Vegetables and entrées, even when cooked a little before serving time, are freshly seasoned at the time of serving to give them an added zest. A good meal is one where everything has been cooked from scratch. Interestingly, even when there are leftovers, they aren't merely given the 'heat and eat' treatment. Usually, they are used as ingredients to rustle up a number of other freshly cooked dishes. Rice is used to make pulav, vegetables are pureed and used as fillings for cutlets, even the humble daal gets added to vegetables to make a different kind of stew. Even cookery shows demonstrate how to use leftovers. For Indians, fresh is wholesome and mostly the real deal. The flip side of this belief—what's frozen and refrigerated is neither as healthy, nor tasty. It stands for a sub-optimal way, a compromise families have to make in today's busy times.

Prerna, a homemaker, can devote time in the kitchen. Working women, on the other hand, who are always pressed for time, prepare masalas, shell peas in advance, and even buy sorted and chopped vegetables if they don't have the time to do it themselves. Sometimes, they even pick up ready-to-eat chapatis if they can't make them at home. But some food, usually the vegetables, is always served fresh and hot. Alternatively, as occupations and preferences free the woman from the daily drill of the kitchen, and as incomes rise, a preferred option is to engage a part-time cook. This option of 'outsourcing' ensures cooking closer to the time of eating, an option much better than the one of using the freezer to store the week's pre-cooked meals.

Rationally speaking, chilling increases the shelf-life of food. Vegetables and meats, when chilled or frozen, can be shipped over longer distances and consumed over a longer period of time. Chilling a food product reduces the risk of bacterial growth. When the temperature is lowered below the freezing point, the growth of micro-organisms decreases rapidly, and will completely cease at a certain temperature. Some modern retailers put in a lot of effort and expense to set up 'cold chains' to ship their fresh produce, and install chillers in the store to sell vegetables. However, none of this matters to the Indian woman for whom the benchmark of fresh vegetables is the push-cart hawker on the street. To her vigilant mind, chilling by modern supermarkets merely masks the staleness of their fresh produce. 'Oh, they have to put it in the chiller, so the "palak" must be yesterday's stock', is how it gets decoded. In the reliable 'warm chain' of the vegetable market, the chilled vegetables 'show up' as stale and are automatically less preferred. Therefore, for the Indian customers, buying at ambient temperature is a more reliable way to buy fresh. Even in supermarkets where retailers stock both frozen and fresh produce, the consumer invariably goes up to the fresh counter even if the vegetables there look a little wilted. But the most preferred option is the street hawker who cannot use the cover even of air-conditioning to mask the 'staleness' of his produce.

Life will change, it always does. Fresh-cart hawkers and fresh fish markets will become less accessible and more expensive over time. We'll use more of our refrigerators for more things, as times progress. But for food brand and factory owners, as well as modern retailers, it's a very pertinent thing to take on board that unlike the west, the Indian preferences will not move to packed and preserved food in the 'cold chain and home freezer' system easily. So what will happen?

Fifteen years later, when Rhea has her own family to look after, won't she become like her mom's western counterpart today? Won't she primarily consume chilled and frozen food? We don't think so. Rhea won't either be like her mom Prerna or Prerna's western contemporary. She will, as a matter of fact, be like Swapna. Necessity will push her towards the frozen section, but her core intuitive preference will always be for fresh. We are still not gazing at a future of frozen TV dinners, something Swapna has never eaten since moving to the US even though it is a widespread concept. Retailers and brand owners who have the courage to stay tuned into the cultural mindset of 'thanda matlab baasi' (cold is stale) and the desire for fresh food, are the ones who are going to be successful in the expanding market for food.

☛ MIND POKE

Google search 'recipes, leftover rice'. While half the world eats rice and therefore has 'leftover rice', the recipes to rework with it and make it refreshingly new and hot are overwhelmingly Indian. Even Chef Sanjeev Kapoor has six of them on YouTube. Try them and tell us how they tasted!

Tell us on the Supermarketwala Facebook page. Please scan the QR Code using your smartphones to take you directly to the Facebook site.

My Own Little Cold Chain

SOMETIMES REVOLUTIONS HAPPEN WHEN we aren't looking. Paradoxically, we don't even know they are revolutions. And we don't realize how our lives have changed just by the introduction of a new product. Indians, especially those born before 1975, talk about the telecom revolution. While lives have changed because of communications, how about the equally significant change in what we consume and the manner in which we consume it? And concomitant with that, how about the way the humble refrigerator has influenced our consumption? Surely it's worth a thought when one single device changes the way a family lives?

Preeti Mehta, a suburban homemaker in Mumbai, started out her married life ten years ago with a 165-liter standard refrigerator. It stocked water, dairy products, eggs, and vegetables. There was just enough space left for cooked leftovers. Life inside the fridge was very humble indeed, just like life outside it. Five years later, Preeti graduated to a 300 liter frost-free behemoth. Even with almost double the space, in no time, Preeti realized that fridges have a magical property of becoming full and crammed for space. The free space allowed Preeti to give full rein to her imagination where food was concerned. Given how Preeti's shopping habits have changed, the full refrigerator is understandable.

Here's what she did with the larger fridge. Some obvious items crept in—more juices, cold drinks, beers, and Breezers, etc. A family-pack of ice cream also found a permanent place. 'Something has improved in recent years, whether with the ice creams or the freezers. Family-pack ice creams now remain soft even when stored for many days,' says Preeti in wonder. No longer was it necessary to buy a half liter bottle of Coke, and wait for it to finish before buying the next one. Now the range and quantity of drinks had increased. And with them, consumption as well. The more variety one saw in the fridge, the more one was tempted to drink.

But even more significantly, the family's adventures with eating out are now becoming experiments at home. Earlier items like paneer, baby corn, mushrooms, frozen peas, coconut milk, chocolate syrup, were all ingredients in restaurant food, and seldom cooked at home. Only the well-to-do could afford to keep up with the latest in culinary trends and stock such items. Now these and other culinary exotica are part of most well-stocked middle class kitchens. Now the Mehta family can indulge in palak paneer or appams for dinner at home, at short notice. Earlier, to cook an exotic meal at home demanded a day's sacrifice to hunt for the right ingredients. Now all Preeti has to do is scrounge around in her freezer, which always has an array of cooked and semi-cooked food items in it. The new refrigerators have changed the meaning of French fries to mean 'open a packet of frozen fries and dip in hot oil', and not 'peel and chop potatoes'. Even recipes now include 'a packet of frozen peas', for example. Diversity at the dinner table is no longer considered exotic or complicated. Stock that behemoth well, and eat what you like when you like.

Clearly, in the last five years, something very interesting has happened to refrigerators in India. Most retailers have probably missed this development, but it can give us some very pertinent pointers to which way the wind is blowing as far as food habits in urban India are concerned. The question to ask is, what, if anything at all, is changing in our lives and the industry as a result of this revolution? The answer lies in the contents of refrigerators across middle-class India, and so that's where our research began. And ended!

Looked closely, there are many indicators of habit change lying there. One of the most significant is around the consumption of milk. The freezer now contains a few polybags of milk, bought at one-go at the local supermarket. These are a replacement for the daily door-delivery of milk that used to be the norm everywhere. So while door-delivery is still how a large percentage of urban homes get their milk, there is now a significant shift in favour of buying two to three days' supply at a time. The delivery charge of one rupee per liter is saved, and the consumer is assured of unadulterated supply. 'Supermarkets,' explains Preeti, 'can be trusted to supply good quality milk. That's not the case with the packets that one gets at the door. And you buy only as much as you consume. You don't have to take the same quantity every day.' Preeti has discovered that the new supermarket stocks polybag milk at a great price. It makes sense to stock it up for three days at a time. The large freezer can easily hold such purchases. Milk in polybags is hygienic and fresh. The convenience of getting it at the local supermarket also means that there's one less unknown factor to deal with. Preeti admits that she has this autonomy only because of the large refrigerator at home. The superior technology combined with the extra space has given the homemaker far greater leeway on how she stocks such consumables.

But let's not get completely carried away. There are still some things in Preeti's life that haven't converted to modern retail. While milk from the local supermarket is now a habit with Preeti, the same isn't true for her vegetable shopping. Ironically, in that department, Preeti places more trust in the neighbourhood vegetable market, which she visits once a week. There are five members in the family, and vegetable consumption is large. It was impossible earlier to stock so many vegetables. Now Preeti is basking in the convenience of shopping for a whole week at one go but not from the supermarket. She refuses to buy fruits and vegetables from its refrigerators. This, she believes, is a way of selling stale food to the non-discerning customer. Of course, there's no difference between the refrigerator at home, and the one in the store, but she doesn't see that! Fresh markets, for the moment, are safe! Things will change in that area also, but that's another subject altogether.

Every other urban middle-class family has bought a new, larger fridge in the last few years. Collectively, we urban Indians buy about 4 million refrigerators—that's a 100 crore-liter 'cold chain capacity'—every year! The total installed refrigerator capacity is 1000 crore liters, and it is growing rapidly. That's a significant cold chain inside our own homes! And that extra large 'cold chain' at home is slowly, but completely changing the way we buy milk, fruits, and vegetables. We're stocking-up more, experimenting more, and investing in more frozen items.

A word of caution here—not everything has changed. Take cooked food, for instance. This takes up the same shelf capacity as in earlier times. Only leftovers are refrigerated. 'Thanda matlab bassi' (cold food is stale) continues to apply. No cooking on weekends for consuming through the week, since we are Indians. Our food always has to be freshly cooked.

Batter, chopped vegetables, kneaded dough, chutney, ginger-garlic pastes, gravy packs, all find increasing space in the cold cupboard—I called them WIP foods (work in process foods). But cooked food made two days back? Not yet! Science may tell us there's nothing wrong with pre-made, refrigerated food, but the cultural imprint on 'fresh, hot, nutritious *khana*' for the family is tough to break.

The new, swanky refrigerator in the middle-class kitchen is giving us some interesting pointers to the ever-changing food habits of Indians. Though new habits are forming, old shibboleths and fixations continue to hold firm. In a way, we aren't changing our eating habits, merely our cooking ones. We are still not ready for ready-to-eat, but we are slowly getting to love our 'ready-to-cook' food. Also taking great pleasure in unloading heaps of shopping bags into our huge refrigerators. Sellers to this category are going to see their fortunes change with our changing habits around the expanding refrigerator. Those marketers who identify the timings of big changes will make us happy as consumers and will make themselves rich in the process!

MIND POKE

It is a fun insight-exercise. Do it at home for yourself. Open the refrigerator and ask, 'What do we have here that we did not keep just a few years back?' Enjoy the discovery and do share your revelations with us!

Tell us on the Supermarketwala Facebook page. Please scan the QR Code using your smartphones to take you directly to the Facebook site.

Thank You Auntie

Indian kitchens outsource more work to other women than to brands and factories

THOUGH CHITRA LOOKED FORWARD to festival time, with its markers of new clothes, firecrackers, visitors, and food, as a working woman she was also stressed by the idea of making the special festival food for her family of four. Her regular office job left her no time to spare for making the *laddoos, karanjis, chakli, puran polis, chivda,* and so on that custom demanded she make, and that her family looked forward to so much. To make all the traditional delicacies, Chitra had to necessarily take time-off from work, something she was loath to do. But she had no choice in the matter.

Her quest began a few weekends before the actual festival as she set out to scour the markets for all the ingredients she required to make the goodies. Lack of practice brought its own set of problems as Chitra laboured through all the recipes, the annual rendering making them inaccurate and difficult to execute. Also, with the new awakening about fitness, there was an imperative to consume less of the fried, sweet snacks. But that's never an option when cooking at home. One inevitably ends up making large quantities that are eventually thrown into the garbage can. Add to this the dilemma of handling the leftover ingredients, special foods like *kopra* (dried coconut) which are otherwise seldom used in the kitchen, but which aren't available in the modest quantity that Chitra actually needed, and the list of wasted food became quite long. It was a thankless task that left her exhausted and anxious. It was also a task from which there was no escape until very recently. Traditional sweet shops do not carry specialty delicacies. Most professional vendors require bulk orders and cater only to parties. So these two sources of readymade snacks were ruled out.

Two years ago, Chitra accidentally found a solution to her problem. Chitra discovered Narmadaben. Narmadaben is a fifty something woman who lives in a *chawl* five minutes away from Chitra's apartment complex. She lost her husband a few years ago, and in order to make ends meet, hit upon the idea of using her cooking skills to her monetary advantage. She had met a few women like Chitra who exhorted her to help them out in the kitchen, and at their request started preparing food for the various festivals that pop up through the year. Narmadaben was happy with the idea of doing this work, for everyone knows that in India festivals and food are inseparable. Whether it is Diwali or Holi, Navratri or Janmashtami, there is always something special that is cooked. Having done this all her life, the older woman had no difficulty in switching to a more commercial mode of production while retaining the traditional taste and flavour. Her 'customers' were happy. For a price almost equal to what they would have paid had they bought all the ingredients separately, they were getting food that would have taken them hours to cook, with the added bonus of being true to the original taste. For Narmadaben, it was not so much a job as a labour of love. She got to do what she was good at and got paid for it.

Chitra enjoyed interacting with Narmadaben. On the eve of Diwali, she went across to 'Narmada Auntie's' house where two more women were working in the spotlessly clean kitchen under the head chef's able guidance. Her host-cum-supplier offered her a cup of tea, and with it some *namkeen*. The latter proved delicious, and without hesitation, Chitra had her pack half a kilo of this along with the rest of the items. Narmadaben, a chatty person, told Chitra many details about the upcoming festival that the latter had been unaware of, having lived in a nuclear family for more than a dozen years now. Chitra could not help but say, 'Thank you, Auntie' as she left with her parcels.

As urban women in India enter the workforce in larger numbers, and migrate to nuclear families, away from the guidance of mothers and grandmothers, their affinity to their culture is also slowly dissipating. A significant manifestation of this is the oblivion into which traditional, time-consuming recipes have been cast. The number of women who retain a significant connect with their heritage and traditions is gradually declining. Nowhere is this more evident than in the way marriages are conducted, with traditional practices being replaced by the mélange of rituals shown on television and Hindi movies. Urban kitchens are also changing, with women seeking convenience and tastes that are more suited to modern lifestyles and palates. They seek conventionality too, but in a form that is more synchronized with modernity. Less and less women want these traditions residing in their kitchens. Instead they prefer the occasional visit! A glaring example is the gradual obsolescence of the stone grinder from kitchens in the South, where many women have even taken to buying readymade idli and dosai batter.

Into this void has walked in a network of 'aunties', women who continue to be connected to their roots in simple, homely ways, can prepare 'grandma's own recipe' for a variety of cooked food, and are willing to exploit this know-how to earn a living. And not just at festival time. Most regular household snacks come from the 'auntie' network. The more organized women are regular suppliers to the friendly neighborhood stores, while the smaller enterprises supply out of their residences. Indeed full hot meals can be obtained from the 'poli-bhaji' (chapatti-curry) kendras, small outlets selling cooked food, that are peppered all over the suburbs in Mumbai, and that are popping up with increased frequency across the country.

As women in the West became busy and prosperous, they adopted ready-to-eat, ready-to-cook meal solutions, branded and made in large food factories. They had no recourse to an 'auntie' network for reasons that are beyond the scope of this article, and large scale industrialization had quickly penetrated the food industry. 'West' thinking multinational and Indian companies have tried to transfer the same technology to India, though with poor success. Ready-to-cook or 'heat and eat' solutions are at the farthest fringe of the family meal at home. This is mainly because the Indian family resists standardization of its tastes and preferences, and moving from its staple meals and homely food to culture-neutral manufactured food is tough. Even in cities, people are still close enough to their roots to know what their traditional food tastes like.

Finally, this is outsourcing country, after all. When the queen of the kitchen becomes busy in the workplace, she outsources her kitchen not to the gigantic food factories, as in the West, but to other women and their kitchen, that is, the 'auntie' network. It is a solution that has proved a win-win for both parties. In this solution, the urban woman is assured of getting familiar and homely food that is fresh and contains no preservatives while being reasonably priced. At the same time, hygiene and purity of ingredients is assured since the food is being cooked in someone's kitchen by someone very much like the woman's own mother or grandmother. For the 'aunties' there is very little barrier to entering this sector. Even the poorest woman in India is trained to cook and bring up children. With their skills in providing processed food solutions that are hygienic, fresh, and customized to suit individual customer taste, these Narmadabens can pose a formidable challenge to the organized, factory-based ready-to-eat segment. Eventually, many of these women will learn to modernize, brand their products and learn to sell them through the upcoming modern chain retailers. When this happens, when availability and close-to-heart solutions come together, processed food will actually enter the urban Indian kitchen in earnest, conclusively leaving behind the made-in-factory solutions. That's the day the Chitras of this world will truly say 'Thank you, Auntie'.

MIND POKE

For several years now I have been helping and keep a strong desire to further help by linking local women food makers with supermarkets by providing them with branding and access to modern stores. Do let me know when you come across any such 'Auntie'. I will be eager to help.

Tell us on the Supermarketwala Facebook page. Please scan the QR Code using your smartphones to take you directly to the Facebook site.

Talk Salad, Eat Samosa

IF A CHEF COMES, can talk of food be far behind? A few days ago, I was at a posh dinner after an art show in Mumbai. One of the guests was celebrity chef Sanjeev Kapoor. It was difficult to avoid overhearing the food related conversation that people indulged in with him, about the easy availability of Japanese seaweed and their recipe for couscous salad and the great quality of herbs at organic food stores. Sanjeev listened to the talk with rapt attention, and then whispered to me with amusement, 'Sab salad aur dressing ki baat kartey hain, par samosa chutney khaate hain (everyone here talks of salads and dressings but prefer to have samosa chutney anyday)!'

Master Chef Sanjeev Kapoor of course didn't mean what he said literally. Burmese khaosuey, Japanese tempuras, and Lebanese babaganoush are regular offerings at parties in upmarket homes. Five years ago one would have had to do a Wikipedia search to find out what quinoa and amaranth mean. Today, any health food fan knows what they are. Sushi kits are hot sellers at exclusive food stores like Foodhall and Nature's Basket. Yes, global food is truly catching on in India and its rising consumption has become an interesting subject of study for marketing pundits, watching consumer behaviour with a hawk-eye. It is an important marker, a badge of sophistication for people who are climbing up the well-being ladder. You 'need to know' how to say 'guacamole' without an accent and 'need to have' avocados and asparagus in your refrigerator, if you want to signal your arrival into the swish upwardly mobile group in the society.

And yet, Indians find it difficult to stay away from their love for samosas and parathas, while also seeking modernity, sophistication, as well as a premium valuation of what they eat and offer. At the most upmarket homes, a cooked breakfast consisting of dishes from around India is the hallmark of an evolved cook. People don't engage chefs, they engage 'maharajs', those doughty men from the interiors of Rajasthan and Uttar Pradesh, who have apprenticed under rustic cooks and are now trained to rustle up delicacies from around the country. Healthy eating with an Indian touch is now almost considered an art form. Stores in South Mumbai, the bastion of the rich and famous, are filled with variants of Indian snacks that are baked, not fried, and give their Western counterparts a solid run for their money. And as far as trends are concerned, where South Mumbai goes, the rest of the country follows. From that point of view, the Indian palate wrapped up in modernity is a recipe for magic, a much bigger magic.

There are many more consumers for an exotic samosa than there are for guacamole, and that is going to remain the case for the foreseeable future. Most local canny vendors of food have already understood this. The other day, I went to buy dhokla from a popular snack shop in the neighbourhood. 'Sir, which dhokla?' was the question tossed at me by the counter girl, who then offered me a taste of the amazing range... cheese dhokla, sandwich dhokla, tiranga, schezwan, crisp and of course, the original khaman dhokla. The most popular varieties were cheese and tiranga! All the fancy new variants were priced 30 percent above the good old khaman; nobody cared. At a recent banquet, I was served traditional Konkani sol kadi in shot glasses. The starters included pav bhaji in martini glasses with a slice of crusty flatbread. These days, I get to enjoy a far wider and more interesting variety of panipuris in all weddings, from different parts of the country, than I have ever done in my life. A recent trend at buffets in five-star hotels is to offer spicy chaat items as part of the salads. Indian street food has been 'discovered' by society all over again, albeit with a more sophisticated twist.

However, despite the strong advent of western influenced food items into the everyday Indian palate, a huge discovery is that traditional Indian food still continues to be the biggest draw at all events. Witness the long queues at the chaat buffets at large parties. Any respectable feast offers Indian food with a twist. So while paneer makhani might have got relegated to the backwaters of Gorakhpur as a premium dish, it hasn't been replaced by canneloni but by paneer coconut gravy, a far less fatty variant. The humble curd rice is now given a star turn at most salad buffets, and is also the first to finish!

If I was looking for a much bigger phenomenon of sophistication of food, and a real mega food business opportunity in India, I should be taking the 'but, eat samosa' hint from Sanjeev Kapoor. Whenever anyone has cracked this magic, a marketing explosion has followed. Who could believe that Chinese noodles could have an Indian taste?

Noodles had an interesting yet distinctly foreign aspect until Nestle's Maggi added the Tastemaker, a wholly Indian flavour, to them, while Lays' Kurkure was all about making the Indian bhujia more sophisticated and 'western'. Smaller entrepreneurs and shopkeepers are also hopping onto this bandwagon. Indian manufacturers like Haldiram's, with their Bisleri water panipuris at their retail outlets and bhelpuri combo packs in modern packaging, have figured which way the wind is blowing.

There is another interesting twist to this story of 'modernisation'. In simpler, less globally linear times, recipe innovation and transmission happened through the conventional, yet powerful channel of granny to mum and aunts to our kitchens. Today this process is too gradual for the rapidly exploding and impatient expectations of the Internet age consumer. Also, with the advent of the nuclear family, the granny connection has watered down. The new recipe and knowledge transmission channels are TV shows, YouTube and Web pages. And the new grannies are celebrity chefs, Google 'uncle' and Wiki 'aunty'. And the consumers are lapping it all up. I love it when I see 'Six interesting things to do with leftover rice', from Sanjeev Kapoor, pop-up on my email. That's six grannies together! I clap when I'm offered the choice of branded Bombay Bhel or masala dosa rolls, neatly modified and packaged, on flights. There's space for a great deal of improvement though, but I'm waiting—not settling for a bland lettuce and mayo sandwich!

The fact is, people want to celebrate their evolving purchasing power and tastes through exotic food, while remaining close to what they have grown up liking. To do this, they need to be helped. And the help is not going to come from small boutiques. As in the case of most consumer products, this also needs the expertise of master chefs, food specialists, large brands, and their product teams to bring in sophistication and bold experimentation. I believe the next level of magic will happen when Maggi aunty, Knorr chachi and Heinz uncle join in the 'samosa sophistication' opportunity. There are some signs. For instance, Pillsbury has just acquired local brand Parampara that makes ready masala mixes. It's a small but emphatic start. A huge branded business opportunity is waiting in the wings. The customer is ready; but I hope the next 'Masala Maggi' makers are listening?

MIND POKE

Sanjeev Kapoor, the well-known chef, is also involved in creating innovative food items and experimenting with fusion foods. Pav Bhaji served in a martini glass, pani puri shots, kahndavi canape's, thalipeeth bites are some of the many starter innovations from his banquet team that I have enjoyed. What have been your experiences with such innovations?

Tell us on the Supermarketwala Facebook page. Please scan the QR Code using your smartphones to take you directly to the Facebook site.

Punjabi Pesarattus and Masala Fajitas

Eating together at home no longer means eating the same food

'BREAKFAST EVERYONE!' SHOUTED SONU Chawla from her kitchen. 'Hot pesarattus.'

'Hot what?' asked her daughter, as she approached the breakfast table.

Dad Deven explained, 'It's just a fancy name for a dosa.'

'You seem to know a lot!' retorted the mother sarcastically, as their maid, Ushatai, brought the steaming, green pancakes to the table. 'Pesarattu, Rhea, is a whole moong based green dosa from Andhra.' She explained, 'Pesar pappu means moong dal. Unlike a regular dosa, this batter needs no fermentation. Pesarattu goes with spicy ginger chutney. Try the chutney!'

Rhea gingerly took a bite of the new dish and grinned. 'It tastes yummy.'

'Mmm...,' agreed Deven. 'Certainly very different from a dosa. Now I know what a pesarattu tastes like, thanks to my Google-happy wife!'

Sundays, says Sonu, are her 'new food' days, when she tries out something new from a recipe that she gets from friends, on the Internet, or sees on TV. It isn't easy to get all the ingredients, though. For the pesarattu, she struck lucky. She got the batter from her supermarket, and the original chutney flavouring was her own contribution to make the dish unique.

Having a full-time maid means that she can do these innovations without too much trouble. It is Ushatai, not Sonu, who brings the hot pancakes to the table. Idlis, pesarattu, kande-pohe, akkuri on toast, Sonu has a whole list of breakfast menus, almost all of them alien to her traditional palate. Indeed, she has come a long way from the days when the Sunday breakfast invariably consisted of dahi and paratha.

Now, every weekend, she makes it a point to try out something new, a phenomenon, she admits freely, that would not be possible without the array of batters, pastes and ingredients that are now available in the retail stores. She couldn't have rustled up the pesarattus had it not been for the convenience of the ready-made batter. The last time she tried to make idlis from scratch, it ended in soggy disasters. Since then, Sonu swears by the idli mix available at the local kirana store. She rues that one can't make kande-pohe from a pre-mixed recipe, but then Ushatai is on hand to do all the hard work, leaving Sonu only with the task of studying the recipe and supervising the end result.

Deven and Sonu live with their 10 year old daughter Rhea in New Bombay. Deven works for a multinational company and Sonu for a high-end architect's firm. They lead busy lives, but Sonu enjoys her periodic kitchen adventures. On weekdays, the kitchen is the domain of Ushatai, and the meals are simple, but hot. But on weekends, Sonu delights in rustling up innovations, a complication that is possible only with Ushatai by her side.

Conventional marketing wisdom says that as more and more urban women like Sonu get qualified and enter employment and as incomes rise, people move to heat and eat convenience foods. In the West, supermarket aisles are laden with TV dinners and convenience food. If everything else fails there are delis offering a variety of cold cuts and salads for the more health conscious.

In India, the reality is proving to have a definite twist, though. The task of providing timely meals to the family, every day, falls on Ushatai, not Sonu. The latter only supports it. Unlike her own mother's days, the kitchen is no longer a place for dutiful cooking—a chore—for the young professional. That part is ably handled by her maid. Sonu 'manages' the responsibility instead of 'doing' it. For Sonu, the kitchen is increasingly a leisure, fun, and skill demonstration place. Weekends and days when she entertains guests at home, are her 'special' days for cooking.

The food adventure at home smoothly swings between ethnic Indian and global cuisines. In the Punjabi Chawla household, bruschettas and pesarattus are equally exotic. They both get their unique 'Sonu' touch, too. Her fajitas with a 'bhuna masala' twist are a rage with their friends.

The Chawlas aren't alone. This phenomenon is now widespread in middle-class India and is opening up a whole new food products market opportunity. When a Punjabi household makes chole-bhature, they start from maida and kabuli chana and cook from scratch. This is what Sonu does because this is what she knows. But when they make appams and avial, they start not from rice and toddy, but from the readymade batter they get from a shop. Coconut milk, for instance, a staple in south Indian cooking, is now available in a packet. The tedium of grating the fruit and extracting the milk is also gone. Ready pastes, recipe masalas, even sambar vegetable kits and Chinese fried-rice vegetables kits, now come packaged and are well accepted. Before the advent of these solutions, Sonu never ventured forth into the unknown terrain of exotic cooking. The only solution was to eat out. But now there is a deluge in terms of what one can cook. Sonu was recently amazed to discover maple syrup at her local grocer. In the past, waffles and maple syrup belonged to the realm of American fiction. Now, they have traveled to Sonu's breakfast table, almost without her noticing the change. Not only that, Sonu has at least three waffle mixes to choose from, one of them a local manufacturer with highly affordable prices.

As food adventures at home take people beyond the known realms of their own ethnic food, they need help with recipes, ingredients, and premixes. These are all items that are bought and not made at home from scratch. However, the vast majority of Indian households still believe in 'creating' as opposed to merely 'consuming'. Anything that 'helps' in cooking is welcome, but ultimately there is no replacement for the oven and stovetop. One can buy dal makhani masala, but there's no question of opening a packet of ready-to-eat dal makhani. This is a fine distinction, albeit quite obvious. Both are value-add and processed foods, but marketers in India can win only with the former.

Misal in non-Maharashtrian homes, cholar daal in non-Bengali homes, dhokla in non-Gujarati homes, is as exotic as lasagne, sushi, or falafel in any of these homes. When these things come home, they will automatically cause a processed food industry and retail boom.

In India it makes more sense for marketers and retailers to cater to the 'choice hungry' trait in families, more than the 'time poor' phenomenon. The emerging middle-class craves variety, and now the Internet makes all of it accessible. Marketers need to move focus to 'add-ons' rather than complete solutions or convenience foods. Convenience foods like frozen pizzas will come into play only when we want a touch of the food-court choice on our dining table—that is when every family member has a particular food preference for a said meal.

My guess is frozen parathas will come to my kitchen not to save time but so that my son can have his favourite mooli parantha while the others can savour their onion, gobhi or any other variant, in the same meal, around the same table. Try making all these paratha types, from scratch, for the same meal at home? No way!

We have a long way to travel before we make the transition to a can and packet based society. In the meantime, it's the people who offer to hold the adventurous woman's hand rather than solve her problems who will win the day.

Maggi Bhuna Masala, Ching's Schezuan Fried Rice Mix, MTR sambhar masala, Smith & Jones ginger-garlic paste - this is what the new India needs. And their sales figures, growing at over 30 percent per annum in recent years, demonstrate this truth ably.

MIND POKE

'Indian Chinese is the only pan-Indian cuisine,' claims the guys from brand Ching's Secret in the piece 'Power Secrets' in the book. Do you agree?

Tell us on the Supermarketwala Facebook page. Please scan the QR Code using your smartphones to take you directly to the Facebook site.

Happy Karwa Chauth!

Festivals bring a built-in 'spending and consumption' licence

RANJIT AND PAYAL SAXENA live in Noida, near Delhi, in a new apartment block. Ranjit is a software consultant with a multinational, while Payal, an engineer herself, is a stay-at-home mom. Apart from everything else, Payal loves Karwa Chauth for the fresh feeni, the thread-like concoction that is soaked in milk and eaten early in the morning. The sweet is available in the shops just a couple of days before this festival and isn't to be seen the rest of the year. Feeni is traditionally eaten by the wife before the start of the day, presumably to ward-off the hunger pangs occasioned by the fast, but the entire family also loves it and joins Payal in the morning to enjoy this delicacy. Feeni is an import from Rajasthan, certainly not native to Punjab and UP, the two largest states where Karwa Chauth is celebrated.

No Holi in the Marwari neighbourhood of Mumbai's Andheri is complete without the traditional thandai, a cooling drink made with exotic ingredients like almonds, black pepper, poppy seeds and crystallised rose petals (gulkand). The Deshpandes in Amravati in Maharashtra always have one dish on the platter on the day of universal fasting: Sankashti—sabudana khichdi. Sabudana, or tapioca sago, was originally an import from distant Tamil Nadu. So, how did it end up in Amravati?

For Satyanarayan puja, a key component is the prasad, the holy offering, which is almost always sheera, made from rava or semolina. The tradition of Satyanarayan puja goes back to a time when the household staples were wheat flour and unrefined jaggery, certainly not semolina and white sugar. These, one would assume, were manufactured products from a distant location and offered to the gods as an exotic food, made especially for this festival. Even little Krishna's favourite food, maakhan misri, comprised homemade butter and big crystal sugar that came originally from Egypt—called Misr in Hindi!

In fact, there's a distinct pattern in the way festivals are celebrated across India. Festivals are and always have been a cultural licence to feast and indulge for the individual and the family. Every celebration is accompanied by food that was once upon a time considered exotic. In the days of cooking at home from scratch with local raw ingredients, fasting items like sabudana, rajgira (amaranth) atta, bhagar (wild rice), sweet potato and festival foods made with besan, maida, dates, sevaiyan, sherbet and exotic fruits, were actually processed in distant factories or imported from far-away places. Weren't they the equivalent of what olives and tofu mean to the young women today, for our great grandmothers way back in that day and age?

Camphor, a vital part of all puja rituals, is of East Asian manufacturing origin. Such items manufactured in distant lands and imported to India must have been really exotic, rare, and expensive at the time of their introduction to our customs. Like silk garments, perfume (attar), and gold ornaments, even these food offerings were probably examples of the best skills and creativity known to communities then. Festivals seem to have been celebrated with the most modern food and offerings of the time. Perhaps the travelling priests of the day became channels for bringing the exotic foods from distant lands and introducing them into the lives of their follower communities. In any case, one fact is obvious—festivals and fasts promoted consumption, trade and modern food habits. All this, with the licence of tradition and offering to god!

However, somewhere down the line, the custom of importing and innovating with exotic things during festivals became stagnant. Now it is no longer considered extraordinary to use semolina for sheera, and sugar is a household staple. But the practice of offering sheera as prasad continues. And yet the hankering to do something new and different on a festival remains. With income growth, prosperity, and confidence all around, there is a renewed eagerness to experiment with ideas and foods. Ten years ago, it was considered cutting edge to have sweets that resembled sliced watermelon. Now, every sweet shop worth its salt offers cashew sweets in different shapes and colours, making the gifting of a box of sweets an exotic affair. The humble clay-diyas, a crucial part of Diwali festivities across India, now come in different shapes and colours, with pre-filled jelly wax to overcome the hassle of making wicks and immersing in oil.

Indians love two things—their festivals and their growing economic status. A typical supermarket trade calendar of a retailer like Reliance has 42 significant regional and national festivals in a year. And they are increasingly learning to merge the two. Indian customs have become even more 'inclusive' and experimental than before. Confident communities will go farther afield to bring in new ideas into the way they celebrate their loud and colourful festivals. No longer do they insist on sticking to traditional formats. The mehndi ceremony has now migrated all the way from the deserts of Rajasthan to the backwaters of Kerala. No urban wedding is complete without a party that is an amalgam of Indian technicolour rituals and western sophistication. Ganesh Chaturthi is celebrated with even more gusto now, and increasingly so by non-Maharashtrians. Traditional modaks are offered alongside kaju katli and chocolate barfi as prasad.

Indians don't need to look any further than their own backyards for the variety of festivals and the myriad ways of celebrating them. And savvy marketers don't need to look any further than these festivals for finding new ways of cashing in. A confectionary company is already doing this in a big way. Chocolate gift boxes have now become a mainstream festival gift, mutating the mithai box, further. Why can't ice-cream manufacturers, for instance, participate in the Kojagiri Poornima of Maharashtra, offering ice-cream 'kheer'? Can't smart retailers promote the Bengali 'Jamaai Shashthi' as the big gifting-day for the son-in-law? With a little insightful marketing, given the Indian proclivity for sticking to culture while accommodating modernity, surely such an approach will be hugely successful? After all, as we discovered, our grannies, egged on by their innovative gurujis, have done it for generations.

Organised markets and organised marketers are slowly entering the Indian mainstream. What better way to seal this 'rishta' than to slide into the culture of festivals? So the next time Payal celebrates Karwa Chauth, perhaps she will get to buy branded feeni and chauth snacks from brand Bikano! And Indians will increasingly wish each other not Happy Valentine's Day, but Happy Karwa Chauth! Happy Karwa Chauth, Payal!

MIND POKE

Can you think of other culturally important foods that are 'imported' for the communities that use them?

Tell us on the Supermarketwala Facebook page. Please scan the QR Code using your smartphones to take you directly to the Facebook site.

[illegible]

Common Indian food [illegible], especially [illegible] foods that are supported for the communities that use them.

PART 4

Fashion Code

Decoding Wardrobes with B.S. Nagesh

IN THE YEAR 1991, Indian fashion witnessed a revolution. In the suburb of Andheri, Mumbai, a department store—Shopper's Stop, led by B.S. Nagesh, opened in the premises of three movie theatres, Ambar, Oscar, and Minor. Shopper's Stop signalled the birth of ready-to-wear or pret-a-porter fashion sold in the modern, self-service way. Suddenly the Indian customer found herself released from the clutches of whimsical tailors and ignorant cloth traders. She could, for almost the first time, walk into a store and experience an array of designs, cuts, fabrics, and colours in both Indian and western wear, try out what she liked, actually, see how the merchandise suited her body structure, without imagining it in a tailor's poky little shop, and walk out with a whole wardrobe that was instantly wearable. No more depending on a tailor's calendar, no more anxiety about the end result! Nagesh remembers those days fondly, 'Liberalisation brought international brands to India, and Shopper's Stop juxtaposed these brands with Indian offerings, all under one roof. Of course, the consumer lapped it up!'

It would be natural to assume that ready-to-wear was here to stay. An array of department stores opened soon after, all of them giving the customer what they thought were unlimited choices. After all, why would she stop getting excited by something that had seemed so path breaking less than a decade ago? But that's exactly what has happened over a period of time—the excitement towards read-to-wear garments has waned.

Nagesh has an explanation for this conundrum, 'Readymade garments, branded jeans, readymade salwar-kameez sets are no longer a novelty,' he explains. 'Every department store offers the same set of variables. It is no longer a competitive advantage to stock this merchandise. The mindset change that department stores like Shopper's Stop brought about is now a given. Unfortunately, stores and fashion houses haven't picked up this reality fast enough. They still operate on the assumption that their merchandise is as exciting to their loyal customer as it was before. They often miss appreciating the vast change in her from even ten years ago. It's ironic that the same stores that brought about a revolution in fashion retailing a few years ago, sometimes find themselves in a rut.'

If tailors are passé and readymade garments are no longer a novelty, what does the future hold for fashion retailers? 'The Indian customer is used to customisation,' says Nagesh. 'She has already bought her regulation two pairs of jeans and a few tops. Now she wants to wear what nobody else is wearing. She still has options of accessible tailoring and seeks the touch of uniqueness and customisation. If her favourite department store doesn't provide it, then she's going to take her wallet elsewhere.'

One of the innovations Shopper's Stop brought in to deliver on this customer desire was to introduce the mix 'n match aisle in the Indian wear section for women. It was a small insight, made possible with only minor variations in merchandising, but it brought huge gains. All modern stores now have a mix 'n' match section that is equal to, if not larger than the pre-matched section of Indian wear.

Another insight that Nagesh offers into the Indian shopping psyche seems almost counterintuitive. 'Traditionally, we believe that the Indian customer is value-conscious, and try to offer her the most optimal price options. However, if you notice, she seldom hesitates to buy a Rs 3000 choli, if it offers sufficient novelty value. She distinctly has higher purchasing power and aspiration. If she knows that nobody else is wearing what she's wearing, she's willing to spend. If we wish to make her more fashionable, to upgrade her tastes, to handhold her overall fashion journey, we'll need to grow beyond seeing ourselves as garment sellers. An all-encompassing fashion business mindset is a better place to start from. We don't realise that with rising incomes (Indians are doubling their income every five years), we are also becoming more assertive consumers. We take pride in our heritage and haven't sold out to the West in anything, fashion or otherwise. What we are looking for is someone to help us merge modern trends with traditional offerings. We must understand that modifying traditions is also as much a sign of modernity as adopting global trends.'

Over time, the consumer in all income and social strata is becoming more fashion conscious. 'It is now normal for the Indian daughter-in-law to wear trendy clothes at home, even in the joint family. Earlier, she wore them only on vacations away from the family. Sarees, blouses, shoes, even gold jewellery, is getting more modern, growing out of traditional designs and being sold at a premium.' According to Nagesh, it is this change that the fashion retailer needs to adapt to. 'Only those fashion sellers whose core point of view connects with the Indian customer will grow faster.'

Another interesting challenge in selling fashion is the physical size of the wardrobe. Paradoxically, while incomes have grown, the wardrobe size has remained the same. Only 10-15 per cent of customers have changed homes and redone their wardrobes in the last 10 years! And all the hangers in those wardrobes are already taken. For sales growth, winning retailers need to put more expensive clothes, more often, on that limited hanger capacity. How do they do that? She was your customer last year, three years back. What makes her come back to you? Does she come to you for her new, higher aspiration fashion, or because she has a higher capacity to pay or does she simply graduate to another retailer? Nagesh often asks his team, 'What's your sales growth by customer household (and not by store)?' Stores need to be loyal to their customers too and move ahead with them to stay relevant. If the customer's aspiration has gone up, the store certainly cannot keep stocking the same merchandise. Also retailers need to encourage and induce people to churn their wardrobes more often—This is not an easy task with the traditionally value conscious Indian customers, many of whom wear clothes till they fade or tear and then famously convert them into mops or doormats. Perhaps all modern retailers will have to handle this problem collectively. In the West, for example, there's a concept of 'colour of the season'. In the summer it might be fuchsia and in the winter it might be something entirely different, grey, for instance. Stores and fashion houses slavishly follow the fashion trends handed down by leading designers and design houses, thus creating a strong market in each season. The Indian market behaves very differently. It isn't beholden to the diktat of the industry. Unlike in the West, people do not get tired of 'colour of the season' here! Their need is for differentiation, not change for the sake of it.

Therefore, the last thing a woman wants to see is another woman wearing the same saree. She herself avoids repetition and if nothing else, will resort to mixing cholis and sarees to achieve variety. In recent years, it has become fashionable to wear unmatched cholis and sarees to imply a variegated wardrobe. In our quest for tradition, the saree has made a comeback, both for formal and office wear. Modern retail, says Nagesh, has eschewed sarees in favour of Western wear, a mistake, in his opinion. Traditional retailers are winning precisely in this area. They offer variety and continuously change to keep up with the times. Modern stores, on the other hand, push for standardisation, a big no especially in women's fashion. The array of the same apparel in a variety of sizes can be a big turn off sometimes. One recent modern retailer that has attempted a different take on this issue, says Nagesh, is Zara. This Spanish fashion retailer has introduced faster, shorter design cycles. So designs change faster, look fresher, and manage to be in-tune with Indian fashion preferences.

In this whole churn, it is the traditional retailers, interestingly, who are becoming more and more proactive. For instance, some fashion and jewellery retailers in the South are adapting their designs to suit modern sensibilities and tastes. Their merchandisers work with the store assistants to pick out designs. This is in sharp contrast to the practice followed in most modern retail houses, where the shop assistant has no say in the selection and purchase of merchandise which is decided strictly by the merchandise department. Corporate merchandisers and designers can pick up some lessons from traditional retailers in this field.

As customers get more confident and economically empowered, they'll assert individual preferences even more and not follow the 'herding' attempts of the industry to drive them into the cycle of spring/summer and autumn/winter trends. Personal occasions like weddings and festivals will be bigger occasions to buy, than fashion industry seasons. Many parts of India have non-seasonal attire. Customers resort to new purchases mostly during festivals, which is when people wear new clothes, and not out of any seasonal compulsion. The same thing holds true for weddings. Entire wardrobes get upgraded during weddings, with every member of the family and even the extended family buying new clothes. One wonders what would happen if the fashion season coincided with the wedding season!

Interestingly, another significant influencing factor for fashion is social media. Earlier what you wore was evaluated only when you wore it and physically arrived at the occasion. Now pictures are instantly uploaded, a lot of times from the fitting room of the store itself, and you don't need to wait to be told if what you're wearing is unique or already seen on someone else's back. In this world of instant sharing, customisation has become almost mandatory. Nobody wants to be told that what she's wearing is yesterday's news.

Real time sharing, comparisons and commenting will force the fashion industry to deliver different things, to Indian customers. Retailers will do well to build flexibility and choice of looks in their fashion designs. It seems more than obvious that new technology will come to the rescue of sellers, who will use it to deliver uniqueness to customers. In a few years, 'only animals will be in herds and follow mass trends; each customer will be unique. Fashionable Indians have always been—unique!' quips Nagesh.

MIND POKE

They say mega retail in the U.S. is fuelled by bigger suburban homes, large cars, and big refrigerators. All these make room for big shopping. What'll be the defining markers for India? What will drive retail trends in smaller cities?

Tell us on the Supermarketwala Facebook page. Please scan the QR Code using your smartphones to take you directly to the Facebook site.

Gold-Collared Men

SANJAY AND ROHAN LIVE with their families in a modern residential complex, in upmarket Versova, in western Mumbai. They often visit the new neighbourhood mall to watch a movie, eat in the food court, and of course, shop. Sanjay likes to check-out the latest trends and colours of the season in apparel, while choosing his formals and casual 'Friday' dressing. The large department store in the mall meets his needs, since it keeps an 'in-season' range most of the time. It is a well-stocked store, and keeps almost all the brands of men's clothing. There are store assistants in most of the aisles and the changing rooms are cool, pleasant places. Almost all of the time, Sanjay is able to refurbish his wardrobe in this store. He is familiar with the merchandise and knows that the brands there follow international trends. The sizes are uniform and the pastel pinstripes and checks conform to his idea of sobriety and trendiness alike.

Rohan, on the other hand, can't find anything to his liking in the hundreds of shelves. He finds the almost uniform colours and patterns indistinct and boring. He wants something that will stand out, preferably in solid colours with a little 'twist' in the design that will make the garment unique. The classy fit and international flavour that most brands advertise is lost on his sensibilities. Everything looks the same to him, and his wardrobe contains almost nothing from the store.

Why does this happen? What is the difference between the two men? They live in the same building, have similar disposable incomes, their children go to the same school and their age difference is negligible. The only difference between the two men is their profession. Sanjay is a senior manager at a private bank, while Rohan is a successful businessman who runs an injection-moulding factory in Vapi. The different professions of the two men lead to vastly different sensibilities and tastes. And nowhere is this more apparent than in their choice of attire.

Clothes speak a lot about the man. We normally think of clothes in the context of women but that's a fallacy. The spate of designers who are now designing exclusively for men is testimony to the rising trend of men wanting more out of their attire than just an elegant covering. Clothes can give an indication even of a man's profession. The American TV show, Suits, is, as the title indicates, all about lawyers. A 'suit' is a derogatory term for someone working for the government and is no longer just an item of clothing. The kind of suit one wears is indicative of the kind of profession one is in.

Fashion, tastes, preferences are means by which we make a statement about ourselves. The white-collared Sanjay and businessman Rohan live in the same building, have similar income levels and send their children to the same school, but what they seek to say about themselves is very different. A peep into their occupations and the dynamics therein could help us understand this phenomenon better. When

Sanjay joined the bank, he entered a well-defined hierarchy that he aspired to climb. He compared designations of his classmates to see where he stood on the corporate ladder.

His desire was to belong, to follow the prevailing norms. Every Sanjay in the white-collared world of banks, multinationals, and large corporate organisations wants to make a statement—he deserves to be there. In dressing and fashion, this is a 'club', and the executive wants to 'belong'. Extend this scenario across the entire white-collared world and you get a class of educated people who follow the same trends—pinstripes, blues and greys, buttoned-down collars, soft colours. It's almost like a uniform, like boys in a premier school. A manager is one who, while leading, also wishes to conform. There is a strong need not to 'stand out' lest one be thought a maverick. Also the banker's calling-card says everything about him. He doesn't need his shirt to do so.

Rohan inhabits a different world where he is the boss. Everyone looks up to him. He has to deal with all manner of people, most of the time on their terms. He has no corporate umbrella protecting him from the vagaries of the Indian system. He needs to exude power, confidence, and an unquestioned authority. He doesn't have a large corporate name or fancy designation on his visiting card and so he needs his own statement of power. This he derives from his clothes, accessories, phones, pens, cars and so on—instruments he uses to signal his distinctive taste, influence, and power. He needs to look distinguished and expensive, and his individuality has to come through. After all, clothes maketh the man. He cannot afford to drown his personality in shirts that can be found in every department store. Ideally his shirts have to be custom-made, but in a world of dwindling services, he needs to find outlets for ready-mades, where he is convinced that no two shirts look the same. He knows that department stores with their emphasis on subtlety and uniformity cannot offer him this reassurance.

The modern department store has still not recognised this fundamental difference between the self-employed and the white-collared. Many marketers make the crucial mistake of treating both as Section A customers. Most corporate fashion houses are inspired by western fashion trends and 'think' about seasons, cuts, designs accordingly. This might have to do with the fact that their leaders, designers, buyers, and marketers, are all from the white-collared world and hardly mingle with self-employed people professionally or socially. At the other end are the fashion designers who tend to ignore the world of professionals when creating their 'look'. As a result, the two worlds hardly meet sartorially.

Twenty years ago, this wasn't the case. Good shirts were either bought on trips to the West or were stitched by experienced tailors. With liberalization, the business manager was relieved to discover that the kind of shirts that he prefers could now be found in his own city. On the other hand, the self-employed wanted a distinctive look, embellishments and Indian motifs. They believed in their own design preferences and refused to follow the style diktat of mass designers. Fortunately for them, there are still some fashion brands that understand this need well. Retailers like Benzer and Chirag Din and brands like Colour Plus are known for catering to the tastes of the self-employed, and successfully so. They offer individuality and the slight flamboyance that almost every self-employed person sports. But are these brands large enough to cater to the entire population of entrepreneurs in this country? And can other brands afford to neglect this target segment?

A recent estimate indicates that in urban India, for every white-collared worker, there are five people with gold-collared tastes and preferences. And like the professionals, this category also has huge spending power. Missing them would therefore mean ignoring a huge slice of the market, and thereby a huge opportunity. If brands truly wish to extend their reach, they'll have to cater to the gold-collared, as we can call them, consumers as well. If they are able to straddle the twin requirements of conformity and flamboyance, they'll have truly made a significant difference to the way apparel is marketed in this country.

One wonders if the large difference in fashion preferences also extends to other spheres? What about entertainment, food, and fashion for other family members? What about the use of credit cards? Running of the household budget? Role of women members in the family? If apparel is so sensitive to a professional outlook, aren't other things of one's life as well? Can the same marketing strategy be applied to all customers, irrespective of the segment? These are some of the questions that will determine which retailers tap a bigger slice of the Indian marketplace.

MIND POKE

Can you tell a gold-collared man from a white-collared man from the clothes they wear? Complete strangers? Accurately? Try it!

Tell us on the Supermarketwala Facebook page. Please scan the QR Code using your smartphones to take you directly to the Facebook site.

The Inevitable Insider

The all-important inevitable insider

'I THINK YOU SHOULD drape this a little lower. It'll suit your height,' said Ashokbhai, the salesman, to Reema, adopting the tone of a confidante. And before long, he took the pink saree from her, pleated it with deft hands and draped it swiftly around her. He tied it at the waist, over her jeans and looked around for approval at Reema's friends, Preety and Pari, who smiled their approval.

The threesome, Reema, Preety, and Pari had come out on that Saturday afternoon to buy sarees for a friend's wedding. As they entered the large reputed saree shop, Ashokbhai, one of the store salesmen, greeted them with a slight nod of his head and welcomed them into the store. 'What type of sarees', 'for what occasion', 'for whom', were questions with which Ashokbhai quickly decided which section of the store was most appropriate for his customers. The young threesome, who moments ago had felt out of place, suddenly got soaked into the smells, colours, and the rustle of silk. Ashokbhai settled them into chairs quickly, all the while silently assessing the seriousness of their intent. From ignoring him, and focusing on the silk stacks ahead, within minutes they were chatting, pointing in different directions, giggling, and deciding their purchase.

Ashokbhai asked them to focus on the fabric and design of each saree. He began suggesting sarees and colours. 'For your height', he said to the tall Reema, 'a broader temple border will look nice'. Reema smiled at her friends. 'What about this colour', he added, 'this looks right for your age and complexion'. Reema was lightly fingering the pale pink and fire coloured silk. A few more options and, 'let me show you,' from Ashokbhai, made Reema see the saree draped around her, rather than viewing it as a swath of fabric arranged fan shaped in the salesman's hands or draped about a mannequin. She modelled for her own saree and was surer about the choice and happier with the result.

Let us note that Ashokbhai was allowed entry by Reema into her personal space. He appeared to have a license to do so, otherwise denied to any other male, a stranger nonetheless, within the short time period of fifteen minutes. Salesmen like Ashokbhai are the 'experts' that convert themselves into the shopper's confidantes. When a woman goes shopping with her friends, her own group and the salesman are the mirrors through which she assesses her purchases. The salesman's feedback carries weight, a privilege denied to other males, even family members. The salesman helps her make up her mind. To get a man's point of view, the woman refers to the salesman more often than to the men in her family. The former, after all, is the expert. Ironically, being a man is an advantage rather than a handicap in this shopping process.

The customer, her friends, and the salesman form a complete evaluation unit, to the exclusion of all others in that store. A curious glance of a fellow-shopper is a breach of privacy, but not the appreciative look of the salesman. He is now an integral part of this team of young women who, outside the store, might not even notice him. He adopts the tone of a confidante when he suggests the cut of the blouse that will suit the saree. The customer and her friends are usually happy to get such advice and grateful for it. The manner and tone are polite; the expression is studied, mainly focused on the saree, the salesman's subject.

Ashokbhai then moved to Preety's saree, and the girls were even more comfortable. He asked Preety whether she planned to drape the saree in a modern style, with the embroidered end of the saree thrown over the shoulder coming all the way in front. Deftly he pulled out a dozen sarees despite murmurs of half-hearted resistance. 'Arre, aap dekhiye—this is our work.' Ashokbhai had judged from the girls' conversation that his customer loved peacock blue and was back to pleating the saree. Soon he draped it about her skirt and Preety was not in the slightest bit uncomfortable as he directed her to tuck it a little lower than the belt of her skirt. He knew that draping a saree was not an everyday event for young women, and a little instruction was needed.

Like Ashokbhai in the saree shop, Lalit Kumar, a peddler in a UP village, gets insider status into Parvati's shopping, when he helps her put on the red and gold glass bangles. Parvati has been buying bangles from Lalit Kumar, who visits the village every other month, for years now. She doesn't feel any hesitation in telling him what she wants when he visits next. Lalit Kumar tries never to forget. He could never cross any bounds of decency with 'didi'. He is visible when needed, turning invisible the moment after the purchase.. Parvati is not uncomfortable under the man's touch as he guides the bangles down her slightly plump hands.

Whether he sells lingerie, sarees, chappals, or gold, the salesman grows within moments of the shopping transaction to become the inevitable insider to the Indian shopper. His ability to strike a conversation, convey a desire to serve her custom, demonstrate understanding and expertise, build trust, and bond with the shopper while becoming her 'looking glass', all these are ingredients in his effort to make a successful sale. Where else does a tradition bound society such as ours allow for the establishment of such quick comfort between genders?

Modern shopping formats growing rapidly in our cities need to recognize this typical ethos of 'personal privacy' in India that includes friends, family and often the inevitable insider, that salesman who becomes a useful close friend, during the sales transaction. The Indian shopper needs and respects the expert advisor. She is used to being understood, pampered and looked after. Will the facelessness of modern stores that allow the shopper so much personal space that it borders on indifference, alienate her at times? Perhaps some store will soon realise that it is worth doing store layouts and trial rooms with a difference, especially for selling ethnic wear to women. We can imagine customers Reema and Preety chatting across the trial room walls. Can there be stores with trial rooms that are shared? Or, in such a shared trial room Ashokbhai can drape the pink silk onto Pari under the participative watch of her friends or her mom? The curious stranger fellow shoppers are kept out; the rest, including Ashokbhai, are insiders. Inevitable and welcome insiders!

MIND POKE

Is the 'inevitable insider' only an Indian phenomenon? Have you come across a different or similar equation in a western country or even an Asian one?

Tell us on the Supermarketwala Facebook page. Please scan the QR Code using your smartphones to take you directly to the Facebook site.

PART 5

Sales Pitch

M.R.P. — Micro Retailer's Poison Price!

'STOP STARING AT MY neck!' says Bollywood star Deepika Padukone to the viewers as the camera pans out from her back to show her drinking Coke from a bottle. 'Look at the neck of the Coke bottle, it's got the M.R.P (Maximum Retail Price) printed on it. Pay that! Don't pay more!' she says. This is supposed to reassure the consumer about the standard price of Coke. In point of fact, India is probably the only market where global brand Coke advertises its price.

The practice of printing M.R.P. on all consumer goods by law is unique to India. And maybe Sri Lanka. As with all good ideas that have outlived their time, M.R.P. too was introduced with the noble intention of protecting the consumer. It was a practice created in the good old days of socialism and controlled production, when demand far exceeded supply. The government introduced the concept of M.R.P. to prevent sellers, the manufacturers, traders, and retailers, from exploiting the hapless buyers who were powerless and vulnerable. A printed M.R.P., technically, was supposed to prevent overcharging. On the face of it, this argument was sound. However, in economics there's a simple mechanism for countering bad practices. It is called the marketplace. The law cannot handle what should be addressed through market mechanisms. Liberalisation was the outcome of this realisation. Over the years India made the transition from a controlled economy to a free market. But some ugly relics of the past remain, and the M.R.P. is one of them.

To consumers, this might seem counter-intuitive. The concept of M.R.P. is a sound one, they would argue. In the absence of a printed price, what is the guarantee that the consumer will not be overcharged? In fact, the guarantee lies in the changed environment that is the retail business today.

Today, frequent shortages of consumer goods and queues for milk and cooking gas are things of the past. Retailers and manufacturers actually woo customers with discounts to get their continued patronage. Earlier a deep discount offer like 'buy one get one free' merited a front page ad in the highest-selling dailies. Now such offers no longer make news. Every brand is jostling for shelf space, and every retailer is struggling to attract customer attention. As consumers get more literate and aware, as competition amongst brands and retailers increases, the power equation turns. Which is precisely what has happened over time in India. Now customers are more powerful and retailers, often vulnerable. In fact, almost all over the world, prices are determined by demand and supply and the guarantee of fair pricing lies in something called free competition.

Even so, what's wrong with having a ceiling on how much a retailer can charge? Why should it be removed if it's not harmful? And why do I call it Micro Retailers Poison Pill? Paradoxically, the M.R.P. is actively harming the small retailers. Let me explain how.

In the old days, when there was no market mechanism

to correct trade practices, the seller made no investment in attracting the buyer. One bought what one could, undeterred by the price or the packaging, in the knowledge that things were hard to come by. Today, the customer is spoilt for choice, and flocks to large supermarkets to avail of the plethora of discounts and offers available there. Given a choice between the local grocer who sells everything at M.R.P. and the chain supermarkets that are present in almost every medium sized town in the country, the customer will choose the latter for their choice, scale, and prices. How will the small retailer make his presence felt in such a situation? It isn't easy but there's a way.

All over the world, small retailers survive because of the services they offer. How often have we ordered a couple of cans of Coke or a loaf of bread from the local kirana store late at night, just before closing time? While the grocer sends these things home, he isn't allowed to charge for this additional service. The dreaded M.R.P. comes in the way. It allows for no premium for services rendered. The small retailer is forced by law to sell goods at the same M.R.P. that your big-box supermarket may charge.

Globally, neighbourhood small stores are called 'convenience stores' and customers know they have to pay for the convenience. As a customer, when you spend time, fuel, energy to drive to a hypermarket in the suburbs, you get things at a discount. And when you are in a hurry, want to shop from the convenience store near home or order from home, you pay a premium. Not in India. Here, now the big-box hypermarkets and discount stores have arrived and they give us deals and discounts. But MRP ensures we don't have to pay any premium when we get the proverbial 'one pack of biscuits or loaf of bread' delivered home. Between the muscular big supermarkets and M.R.P., our friendly old small local kirana will come under survival pressure.

Another change that has happened almost below the radar is the growing unwillingness of small retailers to service orders below a certain quantity. There's a reason for this. Earlier, one could call for even a single item to be delivered. That is no longer the case. This is because the retailer's service costs are changing. The boys who came from the village and worked long hours at subsistence wage are getting scarcer. The retailer has to pay higher salaries. His own family members, his sons and daughters, no longer wish to work in the shop for free, choosing instead to gain an education and work in a professional setup. In such a situation, how will he survive unless his margins go up? The neighbourhood grocer is a part of the service industry and should be allowed to charge for services rendered. Instead, with our insistence on price rigidity, we are forcing him into oblivion. Of course, there might be errant traders who'll charge way above the market price but a free flow of information will push such businesses into oblivion.

As our incomes grow and we start appreciating the convenience more, we'll be willing to pay a premium for good services. For good services to be viable—for Chedda Store to stay open till late, to deliver phone orders and to accept payments by credit cards, old world notions like M.R.P. need to go.

The futility of M.R.P. also lies in the fact that in the poorer households, presumably those that are supposed to benefit the most from having a strict price regime, the percentage of goods with a printed price is much lower than in affluent households. Dry groceries like rice, wheat, pulses, oil, and fresh produce, all the things that have no printed price mechanism, form the bulk of their consumption. M.R.P. is only relevant for branded goods, those that anyway do not play a meaningful role in the overall consumption cycle. On the downside, the M.R.P. is one more law in the government rulebook, one more item of harassment and litigation that helps no one, not even the consumer.

Of course, there are no signs of M.R.P. abolition visible anywhere on the horizon. But I do wonder, in the current era, if there was wisdom in forcing a maximum selling price by law, would not more countries have adopted it? The biggest benefit of an M.R.P.-free regime will be to keep the neighbourhood store viable and available to us for a long time. I can only hope we turn global in this aspect of our shopkeeping soon.

MIND POKE

On this one, I am taking a vote. Not as a consumer, but as a student of retail, do you think phasing out M.R.P is a good idea?

Tell us on the Supermarketwala Facebook page. Please scan the QR Code using your smartphones to take you directly to the Facebook site.

Something About Vendors

WHEN I WAS A young sales manager with Hindustan Unilever in the 1990's, we were working closely with entrepreneur distributors—redistribution stockists, as they were called. Many of the entrepreneurs were from prosperous business communities and for a lot of them, the business had got passed down. We would work closely with them, understand their mode of working and were in many ways responsible for their growth and profitability. Redistribution stockists or RSes sell to wholesalers and also to retailers. In a sense, therefore, RSes are a company's eyes and ears on the ground.

There were two distinct observations that I made about their working.

- They were always short of money in the bank account. Therefore, whenever it was time to pay the company for supplies, the stockists would 'make' large sales bills to some wholesalers, but without shipping any goods. This was the standard trick used frequently to show 'payment received', a euphemism for the stockist's own cash that was deposited in the bank on the day of reckoning
- When I chanced upon the annual tax return of one stockist's firm, it looked like a not-for-profit company! I knew their sales, their costs and could therefore do

a back of the envelope calculation of the net margin. Nonetheless, in their books, while sales ran into multiple crores, with an employee team of over a dozen people, the firm's net profit at the end of the year would be less than a single employee's wages! This was the case for the large majority of trading firm distributors.

Most small and medium business are chronically capital starved (official capital, that is) in India. Decades of high taxes and petty harassments have made income suppression through tweaking books of accounts ('adjustments', in trade parlance) a must-have skill for businessmen in India. As a result, everyone in the distribution chain is always short of working capital. Organised retail, however, is an aberration. Because of its size and more professional and transparent accounting practices, the 'rule' of shortage of working capital isn't applicable. Organised retail, therefore, holds the key to one of the various sales practices that can influence a market—working capital.

Retail managers know that while their official vendors are large multinationals like Procter & Gamble and Hindustan Unilever Limited, what they are actually dealing with is someone like 'Agarwal & Gupta Distributors', the RS of the MNC. And so, while a good relationship with HUL can be developed by promoting their products, the truth is that a good relationship with the RS can be developed mainly by promoting his working capital availability. The RS is not merely a supplier of goods. He is a vital link in the whole retail chain and can be underestimated only at one's peril.

This is exactly what one large retail chain figured out early, and used to get the most amazing competitive advantage. Supermarket retail has a built-in advantage not available to traditional retailers. On the buying end, they buy bigger quantities and get a substantial period of time to make payment to the suppliers compared to smaller retailers, who sometimes have to pay cash on delivery. On the selling side, no customer gets credit at a supermarket. You scan, you bill, you pay and go—that's the supermarket way. For the kirana, however, most regular customers expect a 'khata', a monthly account. Kirana customers buy through the month and pay only at the end. Supermarkets, by design, therefore, buy on liberal credit and sell on cash. Therefore, they are 'cash surplus' on a day-to-day basis. Their competitors, the kirana stores, are not. This particular retailer decided to make the payment terms more favourable to the supplier. So where the industry practice was eight days, this retailer reduced it to four days. In effect, the retailer halved the credit period, thus influencing the vendor's working capital availability favourably. The vendor, in turn, now had a stake in the retailer's growth and continued prosperity. The relationship soon turned into a win-win partnership. The vendor developed ingenious ways to enhance the retailer's market share in various catchments. For instance:

- Promotion stocks came to the retailer ahead of the rest of the market. Also, they usually got an extra lot even after the end of the promotion
- Newly launched products came to the retailer first. The customers got more choice, faster, leading to favourable word-of-mouth publicity
- Local display and consumer sampling budgets were always directed liberally at the retailer
- Vendors ensured that no slow moving inventory was stuck

in the retailer's stores; they wanted nothing to choke the pipeline

- The retailer also received the best in-class margin from the distributor
- If some items were in short supply, the vendor would ensure the retailer was the last one to go out of stock

In effect, the consumers found more products, fresher stocks and more promotions in the retailer's stores compared to the general market. This wasn't something actively created by either the vendors or the retailer, but was a by-product of good trading practices.

Just one move based on a trading community insight—everyone has less money in the bank than needed—hurled the retailer into a virtuous growth cycle, with all the vendors pushing in one direction, with them. Most people in the business would not give a second look at changing these trading practices. If the payment norm is eight days why modify it? Surely the wholesalers, too, know what they're letting themselves in for? And the vast volumes offered by organised retail should offset the stress of extending credit. Isn't that how it works? One retailer managed to peep behind the curtain of wholesaler business practices and understood what a boon more money in the bank was to the trade. And look at the gains they reaped for this seemingly insignificant insight!

Capital formation in the trading sector will lag in India for another generation, in my view. We'll be a capital poor and small enterprise rich economy for many years. While improving the vendors' cash flow isn't critical to a retailer, not in the way pricing, product selection and display, and good marketing is, it carries its own benefits. Once the rest of the retail proposition is in place, this trading practice can give just that little extra edge to the retailer.

MIND POKE

Flip over to the piece 'Simply DMart!' in the book. Do you notice how capital starved vendors were used as an opportunity by DMart?

Tell us on the Supermarketwala Facebook page. Please scan the QR Code using your smartphones to take you directly to the Facebook site.

Thank You Mc Donald's, Welcome Idly Factory

Local flavours at international standards are the best

'SIR, WOULD YOU LIKE your idlis plain, Kanchipuram, or Guntur?' a smartly dressed woman at the counter asks me. I'm in the departure lounge of Hyderabad Airport, and, ready for a quick bite, while I wait for my flight. Usually, I'm confronted with the usual fast food restaurants, McDonald's, KFC, Pizzahut and so on. I indulge in a burger occasionally, though it doesn't really appeal to my palate. This time, I make a tentative move towards the smartly named Idly Factory. It is a new concept—this offering of traditional food in a modern location like an airport—and I'm not too sure about it. But I'm in a mood for adventure, and so I rush in where others before me have feared to tread. Glancing through the witty one line descriptions of each type of idli, I choose the Kanchipuram idlis with a distinct cumin, ginger and pepper flavour.

'One Kanchipuram....,' whispers the server, wearing a smart cap and apron, into a small microphone next to the counter. Turning to me, she asks, 'Today, we have sambar in vengaya Tamil style as well as tomato Kanara style. What would you prefer? And shall I make a combo with filter coffee, buttermilk, or Coke?'

I'm taken aback by the sense of choice, and fumble a

bit before stating my preference, all the time looking at the digital screens behind the server that have the menu, prices, and appetising pictures of the food. I also notice that they have a special takeaway option for idli sambar. As soon as I pay the Rs 110 for my idli-Coke combo, and walk over to the delivery counter, a tray with tissues, Coke and straw is placed there for me. In less than a minute, a plate with freshly steamed Kanchipuram idlis and a bowl of vengaya (small onion) Tamil sambar is on my tray. Next to the delivery counter there's a 'chutney bar' with six types of ethnic dry and wet chutneys. My sense of choice and empowerment, already at a pleasant high, increases dramatically as I help myself to a few of these offerings. On my tray, there is a disposable container of idlis with sambar, another set of small cups for all the chutneys that I collected, a good quality drinking straw, a paper glass of Coke, a disposable spoon, and a few paper napkins. This is the meal that I sit down to enjoy before catching my flight. All around me, there are people with similarly laid out trays, I notice, though the contents are different.

As I enjoy a very fresh, aromatic and tasty idli meal, I notice almost similar sized stalls for a pizza brand, a burger restaurant, and of course, the place I described above—the 'Idly Factory'. In their construction and layout, all the three stalls are nearly identical. An order booking counter with a touchscreen kiosk manned by uniformed youngsters, a visible and transparent kitchen area with gloved and capped staff putting snacks and meals together, disposable containers, tissues, cheerful, and well groomed front teams, bright food pictures, menus, day's specials, and special deals! I smile at the realisation that our humble idli is standing tall alongside the ubiquitous burger patty and pizza base. Burgers and pizzas form the cornerstone of a whole world of food choices, and globally formed modern delivery methods have been created around these to make families feel happy when they have simple, basic, casual food. Even if alien to native culture, international fast food has made a dent in local gastronomic choices by being clean, hygienic, standardised (no matter where you are in the world, a McDonald's burger will always taste the same), and quick.

Global brands like McDonald's and Pizza Hut have taken the casual, functional eating occasions to an excellence level. At a global, cross cultural level, they bring in standardization of products and service, hygiene, transparency of process, branding, and a very modern young ambience. They also establish in our minds a new price point for casual dining—Rs 50 for a simple burger and Rs 100 for a snack meal. We get used to the new price points and with all the excitement, modernity and compelling offers from time to time, we are satisfied with the value we get. Seen in isolation, paying a hundred rupees for a quick snack might not suit every pocket, but customers have learnt to accept that standardisation and professionalism comes with their own costs. A burger and Coke combo in a wayside shack might cost less than McDonald's, but that's not where the hungry Indian middle-class is headed. We are growing to expect quality and learning to pay for it.

At the same time, it is important to realise that no vada-pav or idli eatery, starting from today's Udipi prices, can on its own hope to scale the Rs 40 price point. Those higher price points and we customers who are happy to pay that price, are the contribution of global players in this space.

Until just a few years ago, we were happy with the concept of casual dining equal to street stalls and paid accordingly. Multinational food chains showed us a different world altogether, one of comfortable ambience, low prices, and high hygiene. Ten years ago, these restaurants were crowded with upper middle-class, trendy families. Now the majority of the diners are distinctly middle-class, and it isn't unusual to even see people from the working class enjoying a snack here.

With these new price points as the norm for casual dining, any Udipi diner worth its salt knows that it can create a completely exciting world of taste, ambience, choice, and service. Thanks to McDonald's and its global peers, the customers are more than willing now to pay Rs 100 for an idli and coffee, too. Equally important, casual dining will no longer imply rock bottom prices and squalor. Customers will expect something better and be willing to pay for it.

That's when our Udipis and Darshanis can morph into 'Idli Factorys' or 'Banana Leaf Cafes'. They already know their splendid recipes and fresh food formulae, for generations. They also have a loyal following, developed over decades. Indian food is what Indians want to eat. If they can get it in an international ambience, they will throng these eateries. All that the local restaurants need to do is change their backroom methods a little bit, modernise their serving methods and lo and behold! we have idli-dosa joints, chat, and bhel counters and ice-gola stalls in malls and elsewhere that can pass the global standards with ease. This metamorphosis is becoming increasingly visible. Large local brands, buttressed by the spread of new malls, are now reaching out to the new breed of customers by modernising their entire proposition. There are examples of this everywhere.

At a highway halt in Muzaffarnagar near Delhi, McDonald's and Haldiram's restaurants are located in a common facility. They share a common parking lot, security, rest rooms, and housekeeping services. Both are nicely done-up and have a very modern look about them. Their prices too, are similar. Their menus are completely different, though. Haldiram's even has a special 'Vrat (fasting) menu' during the fasting week of Navratra in North India. This is a popular highway stop for people driving out of Delhi, or into Delhi. The parking lot is full... this place is busy! The point to be noted is that at any hour of the day, the number of people eating at the Haldiram's side of the facility is double the number of people at McDonald's. This is not just true for adults. Children, too, prefer Haldiram's. Clearly, when the ambience and facilities are the same, customers prefer local flavours.

The shape of the Indian casual dining opportunity is now crystal clear. International standards and methods are here to stay. Thank you, McDonald's! And, of course, welcome Idly Factory!

MIND POKE

We want to celebrate and showcase lots of examples of modernising Indian eateries. Send us pictures with a note when you come across a good example.

Tell us on the Supermarketwala Facebook page. Please scan the QR Code using your smartphones to take you directly to the Facebook site.

Chhedda Internet Supermarket.... Now open!

FOR THE WORLD, HEMLATHA Iyer is an e-commerce buyer of train tickets because all her travel is planned on the IRCTC website. The irony is that Iyer Aunty is 63 years old, has a non-smart cell phone and has never been near a computer in her entire life. Her computerised ticket purchase is done through an IRCTC registered agent, located five minutes from her home in Chennai. Mr Thampi, of Rachna Travels, is what Iyer Aunty knows. She gives money to him, and gets a ticket in exchange. What gladdens Hemlatha's heart is that she doesn't have to venture anywhere close to a railway station to buy a ticket, that there are no touts involved, and that she gets a computerised printout, thus assuring her of a reliable transaction without any apprehensions about under-the-table deals. Paradoxically, she also remains blissfully unaware of the technology that underlies the whole convenience. Talk of user id's and passwords unnerve her, while she has never seen a credit card in her entire life, let alone used one.

Rajesh Nair is a frequent traveller to the US, and has used a vending machine there often. It is simple—one drops the money in the allotted slot, presses a button, and hey presto! Out comes a can of soda in the box at the bottom. It is simple, yet every vending machine back home in India has a man next to it, one who takes your money, returns your change, inserts the exact amount in the given slot and presses the right button to get your coffee. All these transactions could just as well be done by Rajesh, but this is how Indians are: they've moved to vending machine coffee, away from the chaiwala, for reasons of assured quality and cleanliness, but they still need a human face next to the machine.

The lesson is clear. We Indians need a computer now, because we know that life is too complex to be left entirely to humans. At the same time, we also need the reassurance of a human interface to guide us through every transaction. While we enjoy the convenience of an e-portal, we don't really trust it with our money. At the same time, we are no longer blind to the sheer range of options that have opened up with e-commerce. Except that it isn't e-commerce as the IT pundits once envisaged.

Mala Biswas lives in Prabhadevi and drives 5 km through narrow lanes to reach Chhedda General Stores every week. It is inconvenient and time-costly to do so, but the quality offered by the store is unmatched. Mala would like nothing better than to order everything she likes over the phone, but there are some items at the upper end of the range that the store doesn't stock. When Mala goes to Chhedda, she also swings by another small shop that sells baked savouries and oatmeal laddoos, almost a staple in Mala's household now. Increasingly Mala wishes that there was some way she could buy what she likes without stirring from her home, a grocery equivalent of IRCTC. All she'd like to do is call, order what she wants and then sit back. Someone should deliver her groceries at home, and take the money from her. Chhedda

Stores delivers at home, but is woefully inadequate when it comes to stocking the latest products with special offers on them. Mala sees these advertised, but by the time she gets them, half of the offers have expired.

Let us see one possible way by which Mala can get what she wants from Chheda Stores. Let's imagine BigGrocery.com. This e-portal for groceries has everything that Mala could wish for, the olive oil and the salsa and the salad dressing and other exotic items, as well as regular use groceries. There are a few of these dotcom services in big cities now and their delivery vans can be seen zipping around occasionally in large metros like Delhi and Mumbai, but there is a gaping hole in their offering—trust. For BigGrocery.com, to gain Mala's trust is a gargantuan task. Chhedda has won it by being around for donkey's years. Trust isn't something that's built overnight. Mr Chhedda knows Mala, and remembers that she asked for a particular brand of olive oil the last time she visited, something he didn't have at the time but does now. He can remind her of that, as well as assure her that his delivery boy will visit only after 7 in the evening, once she's home from work, since her mother-in-law doesn't like to be disturbed. He stocks her preferred brand of bread and tells her when there's a fresh supply of besan laddoos, a favourite with the family. However, he has politely declined to stock the 5 liter can of olive oil or the 10 kg bag of basmati rice that Mala now wants to buy, or the caesar salad dressing, given the increasing consumption at home. There aren't enough takers for such products, Chhedda has informed her. Mala literally finds herself caught between a rock and a hard place. The BigGrocery.com e-portal has everything that she could wish for, but she doesn't wish to interact with its soulless interface. On the other hand, her friendly neighbourhood store is handicapped by a lack of options and the space and capital required for expansion.

Is there a way out that would bring value to Mala while making commercial sense to both the store and the e-portal? It is difficult but not impossible. And the value it will add to the grocery business in India is huge. On the one hand we have e-portals offering groceries online, but handicapped by a sense of their 'facelessness'. On the other hand, we have small stores operating their own version of commerce that's based on trust and relationships but also limited by the range they offer. We can think of a marriage of the two formats. Here's how.

Just as many touts, in the good old days, became IRCTC agents, BigGrocery.com can appoint Chhedda General Stores as its delivery and collection agent. For a small fee, Chhedda can pick up the orders from the customer, fulfil whatever it keeps in its own stock and pass on the rest to the e-portal site. The customer need know nothing of this bifurcation in service. For her, it is a seamless transaction. The same delivery boy continues to visit her, she continues to pay cash and continues to interact with her trusted neighbourhood grocer. All that changes is that now she is given a unique ID number which she has to quote every time she places an order. And instead of getting delivery within two hours, for some products she'll have to wait the mandatory twenty four hours for the order to be processed. What are the chances that the inconvenience of this will be offset by the sheer relief of getting everything from a single location?

There's a sociological reason why this model is more likely to work than the regular e-commerce format. I call this reason 'DIFM'. Indians, while rapidly adopting technology in their personal or work lives, still want things in the 'DIFM—do it for me' way and not 'DIY—do it yourself' way. When it comes to shopping as well, the well-to-do people don't go to stores—the stores come to them. Groceries are ordered on the phone or bought by the household staff, jewellery designs, furniture, and kitchen granite platforms are discussed at home, with the 'experts' visiting home and the customer staying put. As incomes increase even more services—cooking, salon grooming, yoga, tuitions, massage—are being delivered—all DIFM, at home, not DIY!

Even in the west, e-portals are creating robust front-end touch and feel stores. People everywhere aren't comfortable with only an IVR system to share their groceries with. Indians, too have a slightly different approach. They crave the convenience of e-shopping, while being completely unwilling to sacrifice the warmth of human interaction. The difference is, we know we can afford the latter—so why give it up? The beauty of the Chhedda Stores backed by Tata/Ambani/Birla/Biyani is that it panders to this need of customers so beautifully! Perhaps the hour has come for such a service delivery module to evolve in this country. Hopefully, 'Chhedda Internet Supermarket' will open shortly.

MIND POKE

I really want to exchange thoughts with people in India who already buy all their groceries online. Do you?

Tell us on the Supermarketwala Facebook page. Please scan the QR Code using your smartphones to take you directly to the Facebook site.

Coming Soon....Women Shopkeepers!

IF BRITAIN IS A nation of shopkeepers, India is a nation of male shopkeepers. From groceries to lingerie, everything in India is sold by men. Friendly, knowledgeable, patronising, or kindly, but men! This is almost universally true in the country. Wherever one goes—a large metro or a small village—the person behind the counter is always male. This is one field that the sexual revolution has skipped. Women and shopkeeping haven't mixed well so far. In fact, women can be construction or agricultural labourers, managers and receptionists, even priests, but the sight of a woman behind a cash counter is an anomaly that can lead to raised eyebrows. A woman in a shop who isn't the buyer is a curiosity. Barring some categories like fish and flowers sold on the streets, women never traded or 'sold' things to strangers. They didn't 'own' a shop, a place where they exchanged goods for money with the walk-in customers. They sold their services, their skills, managed money or budgets at home, but never got round to selling a cake of soap. To this day, women are hired as store assistants, but very rarely are they the owners. In a small shop, the owner sits at the counter, receiving the money, for the goods sold. Women are seldom seen in this role, even when the store deals in women-specific goods. This is specially true of urban India, where trading is ruled by men.

There's a good reason why. Shopkeeping always involved things only men could do. For example, apart from the customers, the entire shopkeeping ecosystem is male dominated. Everything around a shop is a male bastion. All wholesalers are men. Their staff is male. In a small grocery store, the store has to deal with over 30 suppliers/sales and delivery persons every day - all of whom are rough and tough men. It takes a man to deal with these men. The shopkeeper has to negotiate with them, bond with them, talk the hard talk of 'cash, cheque, with or without bill' and be on back slapping terms with them, to run his shop well. It is hard to imagine a woman doing all this. But to run a shop, all this needs to be done. There is no other way. Secondly, small shops in India are also sweatshops that employ uneducated male workers and children. Women feel threatened in such an overtly male environment. Thirdly, very often shops remain open for long hours, an atmosphere unsuited for women.

Like many other parts of the Indian urban reality, I see some compelling shifts in the way micro retailing is emerging. As these changes flourish, they will lead to us seeing increasing numbers of women shopkeepers in our neighbourhoods, within the next 3-5 years. Women's education, empowerment, exposure are the obvious backdrop for this change, but there are a couple of retail specific changes that are loading the dice in favour of women becoming shopkeepers.

A major change is happening within the store. As small stores increasingly adopt the self-service format, the physical labour of serving the customer gets outsourced to the customer herself. The task of fetching every single item from the racks to the customer simply vanishes with self service retail. This is crucial, especially during peak sales hours when multiple customers can simply 'help themselves' without burdening the shop attendants. Bar-coding, scanning, computerised billing methods make billing and money handling simpler, faster and more accurate. From being a stressed sweatshop with harried shop attendants, the shop turns into a quieter, more organised and less stressful place for the shopkeeper and his/her team. Now that physical labour is no longer an essential part of working in a shop, many small stores in the larger metros have started employing women shop assistants, especially in functions like the cash counters, especially since with computerisation, the owner is no longer required to handle the till himself.

Though this is a visible change in shopkeeping, it is not as major as the one shaping at the sourcing backend. In many pockets of the country, a new type of single point, organised and corporate wholesaler is springing up rapidly. These are the cash and carry stores like Metro, Wal-Mart Best Price, Carrefour, etc. With these stores, buying activity for a small shopkeeper now transforms from handling 30 negotiations a day, with men, to a simple trip to a cash-n-carry wholesaler, which offers transparent prices and business terms for everything a small retail store needs. Also they often deliver to the store – one single point supplier, one creditor, one payment every 2 days! All that a shopkeeper needs is to visit these stores once every few days, and pick up the merchandise. The visiting salesman gets eliminated almost completely! As more and more shopkeepers turn to this method of procurement, the barrier to women dealers is going to collapse. These modern wholesalers are gender-neutral, and at times even biased towards women since a big share of sales staff in these places are themselves women.

So, with the front end of the retail business changing to self service format and backend sourcing changing to the new corporatised distribution and wholesaling model for small retailers, the stage is set for a significant takeover of shopkeeping by women.

Come to think of it, women shopkeepers will be formidable competitors for men. Most customers are women and there will be greater natural empathy at play, if shops are run by women. The locally famous "Ladkiyon waali dukaan" (store of the daughters) in Galla Mandi near Gorakhpur routinely asks its women customers if they are looking for *saunf* for making pickles or for chewing after meals. It'll take a really seasoned man grocer to have the knowledge or the patience to probe such nuances with customers. Amongst today's homemakers, there are so many educated and competent women, who cannot take up formal work because it means commuting away from home and inflexible hours. The option of owning/running a shop near home will bring a large number of women into the economic sphere.

Our field work reveals that most women shopkeepers took to the trade through force of circumstances - husband's death, no one to look after family shop, etc. Gradually, this will become a positive work choice for women, near their homes. It has happened elsewhere in Asia. In Japan and Thailand, between 25-33 percent of neighbouring stores and franchises of 7 Eleven and Lawson corporate chains are owned and run by women.

But how will women build their skills and aptitude for retailing? Most shopkeepers start their 'professional' life as apprentices in shops that belong to a richer relative. After working hard for some years, they finally graduate to owning their own establishment. Men, therefore, learn the trade from a very young age. Women, of course, had no such experience. Until now. Now, girls and 'bahus' are increasingly being inducted into the family shops, perhaps because the boy is busy with higher studies, and labour is increasingly hard to get. Secondly, the new female equivalent of the male apprentice is the store assistant in the organised retail sector, where over 50 percent of the workforce is women. That's where a lot of shopkeeping skills and interest will be developed amongst womenfolk.

A more nuanced but significantly greater tectonic shift will happen within the trading communities in India. These communities are often more conservative and harsh on keeping their women within the confines of the home. Those families who let their women work in their shops, will redouble their business bandwidth, tune their shops with the times much faster and compete well in the era of the modern malls. The trading profession in our country is routinely treated as orthodox and resistant to change. When women begin to emerge from within their homes into the world outside, they will bring social change within their community while creating a better atmosphere in the shop—all the more reason for the retail community to encourage women shopkeepers.

MIND POKE

We want to know every interesting woman shopkeeper, in any kind of shop. We want to support, celebrate and encourage them. Spot one and send us her details along with pictures.

Tell us on the Supermarketwala Facebook page. Please scan the QR Code using your smartphones to take you directly to the Facebook site.

PART 6

Winning Statement

The Wild Success of WildStone

SANDEEP TASKAR IS A sales executive in a plastic manufacturing unit in Mumbai. Sandip lives in the far suburb of Dombivli and goes to work in Andheri, a two-hour transit. Sandip likes his job and doesn't mind the long hours or tedious commute. 'The pay is good,' he explains, 'and I enjoy the task of selling. I love meeting people and convincing them to buy from me. I started working eight years ago, immediately after graduation. Since then I've made decent money, enough to afford the better things in life.' He brandishes a can of deodorant (deo) spray as he says this, grinning all the time. 'I started using this about two years ago. I didn't realise deos can be so useful in controlling sweating and keeping me feeling fresh. Earlier, I used to think only the rich kids use deos, but now I can't do without one myself.'

Before the recent flurry of activity, the perfume market in India was limited to a few imported brands of eau de cologne or very high-end perfumes. One of the early full-blooded entrants in the deo category was Axe by Unilever. Deo brands are sold with a lot of imagery and advertising around the brand. The Axe imagery was one of posh, college-kid sexiness—young, rich guys overwhelming immensely beautiful, fantasy women with their perfumed aura. The brand appealed to youngsters and found a market in the metros, especially amongst the upper middle-classes.

N.K. Daga, a distributor of many FMCG products in Kolkata, had a different perspective on the market for perfumes in India. He knew, through his experience in the dusty streets of east Indian towns, that there was a resurgence, and the Indian youth was transforming itself into an aspirational class. They were coming into money for the first time ever and they were looking for ways to spend it. Any marketer, who understood that consumption wasn't restricted to the creamy layer, was going to hit the gold mine called the Indian middle-class.

The deo market in India was rising out of almost thin air. While Axe was the market leader, and a couple of other multinationals had taken baby steps in this country, Daga knew that they had merely scratched the surface of the market, that there was a whole generation out there that wanted to acquire a deo, but didn't believe that a 'rich man's deo' would suit their taste. Daga saw an opportunity and decided to make the most of it.

Daga, with his canny business instincts and ear to the ground, knew that he wasn't in the market to create a 'me too' product. He could improve upon the international imagery of Axe and did so. The Indian sensibility appreciates stronger perfume, and equates it with a 'better' product, and Daga's deo had just that. As far as the price was concerned, Wild Stone wasn't going to be seen as a cheap variant. Low price and poor quality are often correlated in the mind of the customer, and it would be a paradox to offer a better product, priced cheaply. Daga decided to exploit the weakest link in the Axe chain, its positioning. How did he do this?

The Indian sensibility towards romance, in small towns' and suburbia, is nuanced with shyness and innuendo. Men and women maintain a distance from each other, and yet play the courting game through smiles, glances, and in extreme cases, a very brief touch. There's no question of privacy, of being sequestered in a room together, and the concept of sexual liberation is still not a mainstream phenomenon. The sexual overtones of a regular deo ad would have limited appeal in a market where romance is still linked to the covert. 'It is in this very Indian space that my brand Wild Stone resided, as it grew from strength to strength,' says the mild-mannered Kolkata man behind the brand that is amongst the top deo and perfumes brand in India today. Barring the states of South India, where the brand has low presence, most markets it operates in, Wild Stone has climbed up to market shares above seven percent, going as high as 12 percent, ahead of many global brands. If marketing creates meaning around products and sharp clarity on the role of the brand shapes winning brands, Wild Stone's story is as good an example of good marketing as you can get. If you search for 'Wild Stone, Aqua Fresh ad' on YouTube, the TV advertisement lives the role of the brand to the last detail. There is no in-your-face 'get the girl' plot. There are no Western models or college romance storyline. Instead we are given the merest hint of attraction between a sari-clad woman and a man sitting on the adjoining roof in a very small town 'mohalla' type of setting. Nothing could better communicate the Indian ethos of the brand.

This is not a deo, the advertising seems to communicate, that is only meant for college kids with more liberated and individualistic thinking.

As more consumers in India get aspirational, as deos reach deeper in consumer usage, a large number of new consumers relate to stories that spring from the real Indian milieu. There will always be a segment of the market that would relate to and consume entertainment, advertising, and brands with global ethos. Given the nature of the market, though—to give a Mumbai analogy—eventually Malad and Borivili, the more middle-class suburbs, will be much bigger markets than their richer neighbour, Bandra, can ever be. The real big, aspiring India relates to the Wild Stone-way of talking, more than the global way of talking personal products.

As modern fashion stores and supermarkets go deeper into India, they'll provide a superior showcase for brands like Wild Stone that tell a new story. The modern store phenomenon will help them rise on the popularity charts faster. To a large number of new consumers even a good product and a rational story would appeal. Personal products like deodorants, skin creams sell a lot on a distinct story and image that surrounds the brands. For brands that get their story right, modern retail provides a golden opportunity to showcase their products and reach it to the market faster. The display mode of selling that is modern retail will always be advantageous to new comers. A story that connects faster with the Indian consumer and stores that showcase the products better, there can't be a more powerful symbiotic platform for expansion of many new categories.

How entrenched are Indian cultural preferences? Quite, as Daga narrates, regretfully. Customers were comfortable when the edginess in the ads stopped at the boundary of a teasing, tempting type of seduction. When another Wild Stone TV commercial crossed the line and actually depicted illicit behaviour, the ad was disliked, and rejected. Search YouTube for the Wild Stone Hunt ad, to know the difference. For Daga the lesson was stark. If you wish to show real Indian imagery and stories, you need to stay sensitive to cultural boundaries of behaviour, beyond which, people get turned-off. This, as we have read before, is an asserting market with deep-rooted preferences.

Brand Wild Stone has a unique capability by its side as it propagates its products and distribution reaches deeper into the Indian market, on its edgy positioning. It has crafted all expressions of the brand—from packaging to advertising, to point of sale, and even digital media presence in-tune with its 'Indianness'.

For the marketing fraternity, the journey of brands like WildStone will decide how brands will talk a distinct Indian story and not merely mimic or ape what's been said in culturally very different places—otherwise known as the global markets!

MIND POKE

Catch all the innovative Wild Stone ads on You Tube as per their appearance, and spot with which advertisement campaign the company changed its ad agency?

Tell us on the Supermarketwala Facebook page. Please scan the QR Code using your smartphones to take you directly to the Facebook site.

Simple, DMart!

RITU BHATTACHARJEE WORKS AS a sales executive at an automobile dealership in South Mumbai and lives with her husband and six year old son in Powai, in the geographical centre of Mumbai. 'I love it here!' she says. 'There is nothing that is not available in our neighbourhood. Restaurants, stores, cafes, bookshops, everything is just a two-minute walk away from our place. And ever since DMart opened, life is perfect. I don't have to go anywhere else for grocery shopping.' When asked about another supermarket close by that pre-existed DMart, she dismisses it with a wave of a hand. 'They don't stock many things that I want. But DMart does! Sometimes I wonder if they've placed a spycam inside my house. How do they know exactly what I'm looking for?' she laughs.

Ritu is one amongst thousands of women in the city of Mumbai and now, other cities as well, who find not just satisfaction, but actual deliverance in DMart. They have no hesitation in extolling its virtues. And their praise is almost identical. 'DMart has everything we want. The offers at DMart are unbelievable.'

'This is the only supermarket in India where the customer is not bothered about the ambience of the store. Her entire attention is centred on filling-up her shopping-trolley without a care in the world,' said an employee in a leadership role at Wal-Mart, after visiting a DMart store in Mumbai in 2008. 'We know for a fact that when a customer is completely sure she is getting the best value, she lets her guard down, she buys more and in the bargain, the store wins,' he puns with a deadpan face.

DMart wasn't conceived through a grand business strategy, but merely as a hunch that was backed by its promoter, R. K. Damani. And yet, it is acknowledged as a successful, solid, home-grown, regional supermarket chain in India. It stands tall amongst large corporate and multinational supermarket chains, in its areas of operation. How did this happen? How did a humble, unadvertised, unsung, and relatively unplanned venture do better than its more organised competitors? How does it remain the market leader in its catchments year after year? Obviously, there is something this supermarket does smarter than many bigger, wiser supermarket teams.

The story of DMart began almost fourteen years ago in the dusty streets of Mumbai and upcountry Maharashtra where its promoters walked the supermarkets and co-operative stores of the time and observed the contents of the shopping trolleys to gain an understanding of what the customer bought and what she rejected. All operational wisdom was gleaned from the supermarket 'street', while philosophically, it was clear that the store must follow the principles laid down by Sam Walton, the fabled founder of the global retail giant Wal-Mart. Wal-Mart had treated some fundamentals as gospel and if they could succeed with their simple approach to retail, there was no reason for a store in India not to do so. In a very basic way, therefore, all DMart did was to watch the customer trolley and read everything about Sam Walton and Wal-Mart. Nothing else was strategically important. The strategy paid-off in spades. DMart's 'Give 'em what they want' approach to retailing has customers lining up at their doors.

Our work at understanding and decoding DMart led to some simple clues and points of view about each of the three constituencies of retail—the customers, the vendors, and the employees.

DMart started in a very simple way in New Bombay. By supermarket standards, the first store, which also acted as a pilot for the business, located in a 4000-square feet premises, was tiny. But the principles it developed then have stood the test of both time and scale. The business was in no hurry to create behemoths. Instead it patiently went about laying down the first principles of this fledgling business, and creating the core DMart point of view about the three 'constituencies' of retail. Now the simple formula that makes DMart tick is shared and intuitively understood as invaluable in the large organisation. Probably this simplicity has helped it scale nicely, while staying lean as an organisation. One of the cornerstones of DMart's continued success is how it has retained its frugal outlook to retail through all market upheavals and internal changes over the years.

From his stock investor days, R. K. Damani, or RK, as he is popularly known, had the habit of forming strong, informed points of view about what mattered for success and single-mindedly pursuing the chosen path. He pursued the same mindset in the retail business. One of his biggest success sutras was that of prioritising with a vengeance. 'If there are ten principles or acts needed to run the business, I would pick the two or three that mattered most and then drive them to be a market beater in those areas. I am fine if in the other seven areas I am considered below average,' he says confidently. Running with what matters the most and staying the course has obviously been a winning strategy for DMart. It is therefore worth examining the most important components of each of the three constituencies, the customer, the employee and the vendor, for DMart.

The DMart point of view for the three constituencies

1. **The Indian customer**, who shops at air-conditioned stores, does not run her family's grocery needs on a tight budget. While supermarket customers are, by and large, well-to-do people, yet everyone wants to save money. People with money buy more, to achieve higher savings. DMart's pricing is designed for the customers to save more across everything she buys. However, those who buy bigger packs, save even more. It's as simple as that! The merchandise department of DMart, its buyers, act more like agents of the customer and not of the company. This is in line with Sam Walton's description of his merchandise department. If the buyers buy better, they can sell cheaper. The very fundamental principle of 'what you receive, you pass on' is almost biblical in its simplicity. If buyers negotiate a good price with vendors, DMart passes on the benefits to the customers, in the process, communicating a message of care and protection. 'Even when you are not looking, not careful,

you'll still save money with us' seems to be the unstated subtext in its communication. How can any customer resist such a message of genuine concern? It follows that the customer will let her guard down and fill her trolley with reckless abandon. After all DMart has her back and she knows it. One of RK's old beliefs is, if she saves well, she'll overlook other flaws in the offering. There are many aspects to a customer facing business. A well-lit and designed shop-floor with smart adjacencies and category flows, polite staff, proper communication, attractive displays, weekly, monthly promotion cycles, so on, and so forth. DMart could have tried to focus on all these and more. It didn't because then it would have lost its edge. It only looked at how much the customer saves, and became a market leader in that, much to the shopper's joy. She bought more. 'Also, she'll tell others about us and therefore we'll not need any marketing!' chuckles RK.

2. **Store employees or associates** are first generation retail workers in India. Self-service retail is still in its early stages of evolution here. Combine this with the fact that culturally, in India, service and servitude have often been treated as one and the same, and it becomes obvious that introducing a service-oriented format in our country is a mammoth task. Workers and servers in all walks of life come from a different class and socio-economic background than the people they serve. They are largely untrained and often uneducated or first generation learners, their parents being employed in small factories or as work hands in small businesses. Nothing in the environment or upbringing of these new retail associates

therefore, prepares them for a customer-facing service job. The service culture is entering our environment, but it will take a generation to become firmly entrenched as part of our society. Until that happens, what is a customer-facing business to do? Can it afford to depend on this class of workers to generate customer satisfaction? The obvious answer is no. From this point of view, DMart has built a cadre of simple, hardworking store people, who ensure fully stocked shelves, clean price communication, and efficient check-outs and not much beyond in customer service. Well, selling simple grocery items at fixed prices does not require much people-based service, in any case. The simplicity of the shop-floor associates is offset by state-of-the-art, global standard store equipment. Be it flooring, shelves, trolleys, scanners—all hardware and connectivity deployed at the stores is expensive, best in class. Not many things therefore need skilled, smart manpower. Equally significantly, the associates have no sales targets. Clearly, the organisation does not depend on its associates for its sales. It allows its systems and basic principle of simplicity to do that for it. DMart seems to live its 'self-service' dharna, diligently. While staff are amply trained and rewarded, this is not where the company has chosen to place its sales focus on.

3. **Vendors**, who deliver goods and get paid by retailers, are small and medium traders, micro-entrepreneurs, by a vast majority. Even when supermarkets buy goods made by reputed MNCs, the real last-mile seller is often a distributor named Agarwal & Sons, for example. Small traders in India, as a rule, are always short on capital and

perpetually stressed about their working capital situation. DMart decided to be a market beater by paying faster than market norms to its vendors. Quickly, they became known as the best pay masters in town. In spite of being tough negotiators, every vendor wanted them to succeed, for this very reason. Vendors did many small things in their power to ensure DMart got the best availability and deals. Vendors are known to advise and tip-off the buyer teams, often, with market intelligence. DMart has ensured an ecosystem that's very helpful in winning the complexities of the supermarket business, with this simple vendor insight. It also helps to have a liberal stock holding policy the way DMart does, in a growing market like India.

The Indian customer is intuitively frugal and also traditionally underserved. When she sees a hardworking store like DMart that empowers her, saves her money, and has a no-nonsense outlook, she overlooks and forgives the no frills, often cheerless, warehouse like store setting.

Going forward, from being a regional retailer, as it expands into other parts of the country, DMart has to grapple with the fact that India is more like a continent than a homogeneous market. Food tastes and preferences and buying behaviour change every 100 kilometres. Assortments, work cultures, and therefore overall management will need to get complex. A simple business model based on insights about the three constituencies of retail and a trusting, forgiving customer will stand in good stead when DMart begins to engage with greater complexity.

It is a well-known fact that in most large markets, the

biggest retailer is the discount supermarket and in many cases it is a local player and not a multinational. DMart with its stable fundamentals is well-placed to play for that spot, for now at least!

MIND POKE

There are many regional gems amongst modern retailers in India. I believe they are a treasure trove of good practices. Pothy's, Pazhamudir Nilayam, Sarvana Stores in Chennai, Jalan's in Varanasi, Sarvodaya in Mumbai, and Khadim's in the east are some gems that come to mind. Which are the other such great retailers that you have come across?

Tell us on the Supermarketwala Facebook page. Please scan the QR Code using your smartphones to take you directly to the Facebook site.

Powerful Ching's Secrets

SO HERE'S A TRICK question: Which is the cuisine with a uniformly high pan-Indian appeal? In other words, which type of cuisine can now be found all across the country and has a uniform acceptance rate? All popular foods that can be found across India have a distinct regional bias—idli, naan, chicken tikka, rosogulla—the appeal decreases as you travel away from their region of origin. Idlis are now a common snack everywhere but nowhere as popular as in the South. Every Bengali will testify that the best rosogullas can be had only in Bengal. They might be a common sight in most sweet shops, but their acceptance is highest in the East. So what's the right answer to the trick question? Ajay Gupta, a food entrepreneur from Mumbai, had asked me the question about the truly pan-Indian cuisine. When he saw my confusion, his tongue-in-cheek but accurate answer was, 'Indian Chinese. Indian Chinese is popular as street food, restaurant fare, and now also at home, across the country, from Aizawl to Jaisalmer and from Leh to Quilon,' he chuckled.

He should know, for Ajay has been selling the Ching's Secret brand of Chinese food products for fifteen years in India. When he launched the brand, he clearly saw the popularity of Chinese food in India.

Indian Chinese is a unique hybrid cuisine. Ask any Chinese worth their ajinomoto and they will not have anything to do with what passes for Chinese food in India. In fact, a word has already been coined for this food. It's called 'Chindian' food. Perhaps it was born out of several influences in India, the Tibetan and the Northeastern or the early Hakka settlers in Kolkata, for instance. Ajay and his brand, Ching's Secret, wish to popularize it as Hakka Chinese cuisine. Clearly, it isn't Chinese food the way the Chinese make it, but it is the way Indians make it. Just as a Domino's pizza is a far cry from a real Italian pizza, but has emerged out of the American palate, Indian Chinese food is an outcome of the differently designed Indian palate. This is clear from the very different Chinese food that one gets in upmarket Indian restaurants. The Chinese food that the average Indian consumer is looking for is a very different cup of tea, however!

Indian Chinese restaurants had already gained popularity when Ching's Secret started its journey. One can safely say that after mainstream Indian restaurants, it was the Chinese restaurants that were the most popular, and still are, as a matter of fact. In the old economy days, when fine-dining was far rarer than it is today, people considered it a badge of honour to tuck into their chicken chowmein and wonton soup. All dining neighborhoods sported a Chinese and a Punjabi food restaurant. Other cuisines had yet to make an entry into the fine-dining scene, and were therefore missing from Indian kitchens as well.

As a food entrepreneur, Ajay smelled an opportunity there. Maggi noodles, the forerunner of all ready-to-eat noodles, had already created a minor storm in the food industry. Ajay, however, was clear that that wasn't the direction he wanted to move in. Maggi was positioned as a children's snack. What about the rest of the family? What did it turn to when it wanted to 'be exotic'? And this is where Ajay's understanding of the middle-class Indian woman became the trigger for his success mantra.

'The Indian woman will eat out with the family. After three or four such outings, which are as much outing as a tasting opportunity, she replicates the same menu, at home. Take-out is a big no-no for the proud Indian homemaker. And eating out has increased, but is merely a leisure activity, not a replacement for the meal at home. It is not enough to simply enjoy an exotic meal cooked by someone else. Indian women are invested in proving their prowess in the kitchen. Most of them think of themselves as quasi-chefs. They do that with pizza, chole bhature, Thai curry, Hakka noodles, and Schezwan fried rice. I designed brand Ching's to provide a little crucial help to the Indian woman to win with her family in this quest.' Ching's secret was this—the Indian woman could do with help and not with a replacement for her skills in the kitchen. This is exactly what Ajay set out to do. He didn't seek to become the Cup o' Noodles. He knew that that was always going to be a niche opportunity with Indian homes. And the value conscious Indian consumer wasn't ready to pay a premium for convenience. The kitchen shelf needed a few allies. It was Ajay's job to identify and provide them.

The Ching's Secret range includes Hakka noodles, soya sauce, chili sauce, soup mixes, and magic masala for fried rice. Each one comes in variants such as Manchurian,

Schezwan, and hot garlic. The heart of Ching's Secret does not lie in the 'simply heat and serve' products that even unskilled men can prepare and serve. Ching's Secret makes sure 'every homemaker gets her Chinese cooking right every time, even as she adds her unique touch to it. She has to be the architect in the kitchen, the one who designs the food and finally brings it to the table. She has no desire for quick fixes,' points out Ajay.

While the insight into the Indian food psyche was the linchpin of Ajay's entire business strategy, that wasn't the complete story.

Capital Foods, the parent company for Ching's Secret, started life as a food export company to the American and European markets. At the very outset, the company invested in state-of-the-art, globally certified plant and machinery. 'Our exports business of frozen parathas and a dozen other Indian dishes to the US and European markets taught us the importance of food-safety standards. Even when we were small, our plants for Ching's Secret were globally certified and export-worthy. It helped us deliver to our local Indian customers the trust of consistent quality, so important with food brands,' declares Ajay. By not taking shortcuts in manufacturing, Ching's Secret could afford to dream big. Ajay knew that food manufacturing was a sensitive business and made the right strategic decisions on that front.

Now Ching's Secret knew what to make and how to make it. The technology and product were in place. But all the technology and product insight would have fallen flat on its face, were it not for the advent of a major revolution in Indian retail, the modern, self-service supermarket. What was the connection?

'The biggest hurdle for the start-up entrepreneur is the marketing challenge. How does one reach the eyes and ears of the millions of consumers out there? And how does one stand out in the crowd? This is where modern retail helped me. The self-service supermarkets became my marketing, advertising-cum-distribution channels,' says Ajay, remembering the year 2002, when he personally supervised demonstration and sampling of freshly cooked Hakka noodles and fried rice in supermarkets. 'Traditional retail has no space for newcomers like me,' he goes on to explain. 'The challenge is to get noticed. Marketing campaigns need big budgets, something I didn't possess. How was I going to circumvent this problem? I had no money for television advertising. At the same time, I was convinced that I was sitting on a great idea, that my product was ideally suited to the Indian palate. Then it occurred to me that the most obvious thing to do was to induce trial through sampling. Once the customer tasted my product, I was sure of converting her. But the question was how to do the sampling? Traditional grocery stores couldn't offer me adequate space for this experiment. Also the footfalls at these stores were fewer and scattered, and the effort required to set up the sampling was huge compared to the returns. This is where modern retail came to my rescue. The stores were large, invited significant numbers of customers and were willing to partner with me in trying out a new marketing strategy. The open shelves and the attractive offers worked as my ads,' he says. 'I could send out my brand proposition through these shelves without having to spend big money on conventional advertising.'

To add to the charisma of the brand, Ajay decided to

explore one more aspect of the middle-class Indian kitchen. While the woman of the house wanted to be adventurous in her cooking, she had no idea what this entailed. For instance, most women were aware of Hakka noodles as one of the chief dishes of a Chinese meal, but not what went with it. Was it enough to have a sweet and sour vegetable? Was something more required? Ching's Secret found itself in the position of not merely an innovator, but a mentor. When one of the largest retailers in the country suggested that Ching's Secret present itself as a total solution, Ajay knew exactly what he should do. And since this retailer was a brand partner as well, Ajay got the freedom to represent all Chinese cuisine ingredients together on the shelf as a single section. Now the customer saw not Ching's Secret Hakka noodles in one aisle and Ching's Secret soya sauce in another, but the entire range together, at one single place. The power of suggestion became a multiplier in itself. The supermarket shelves 'told' the customer to buy sweet corn soup to go along with the main meal. Ching's Secret no longer stood for 'ingredients for Chinese cooking', but a do-it-yourself Chinese menu. The product range opened the door for any woman who wished to prepare a full Indian Chinese meal at home. No wonder the brand succeeded in the face of giants like Knorr and Maggi. The difference between them and Ching's was that while they offered a product, Ching's—the Chinese expert—offered a cuisine solution.

Today the brand advertises on TV, was a sponsor for the popular reality show, Indian Idol, sells in both urban and rural markets and has a huge presence in all kirana stores, but Ching's Secret was probably the first mainstream brand in India that was built in modern retail stores and then moved to traditional retail. It successfully tapped into the access and depth of the large, self-service supermarkets, and capitalized on the growth these offered to its advantage. The mantra of Ching's Secret's success is now being replicated by other new-age marketers, who are following the trajectory it pioneered, of cutting its teeth in modern retail and then fanning out to the traditional channels.

How successful is Ching's Secret as a brand? One hint that we have lies in its sheer reach. It has cut into the slums of Dharavi, a primarily lower middle-class neighbourhood, where its sachet packs are flying off the shelves, proving that the newest addition to Indian cuisine is Chinese food, even in modest homes. At the same time, the global Indian diaspora, which craves all things 'desi', can now spot Ching's Secret on the shelves of Loblaw, the largest food retailer in Canada.

Ching's Secret's overwhelming success is founded on the bedrock of empathy, a firm hold on what the Indian customer is looking for. More than any other aspect, it is this understanding that has given the brand such a solid foundation. How many multinationals can claim this crown? The answer is obvious—too few.

MIND POKE

I would imagine Idli-Dosa made from ready-to-cook batter is the next pan-Indian food waiting to happen in our homes. Do you agree? Or do you think that mantle belongs to some other food/cuisine?

Tell us on the Supermarketwala Facebook page. Please scan the QR Code using your smartphones to take you directly to the Facebook site.

Talwalkar's For Women!

AT A TIME WHEN fitness and 'bodybuilding' were synonymous and therefore were restricted to poor, young men with their 'akhadas' and 'vyayamshalas', Vishnupant Talwalkar's decision to open a gym in the year 1932 was revolutionary and in total contrast to family wisdom. The so-called upper middle-class, 'decent' families, did not voluntarily become associated with this business. Fitness wasn't considered necessary, unless one was associated with 'physical' professions, those that involved violence or muscle power. But Talwalkar was a visionary and knew that the country, especially its middle-class, needed professional help to stay healthy and strong. He stuck to his guns, and opened his first gyms in the middle-class neighbourhoods of Khar and Charni Road in Mumbai. However, it soon became clear to the man that unless he created a unique positioning for his gyms, they would be perceived akin to 'akharas' by his customers. The answer to this problem soon became obvious. 'Akharas' were where only men went; therefore gyms had to be where females could also go. In 1943, when Talwalkar invited his members to bring their women to join his gym, this insight was nothing short of revolutionary. Women, at the time, leading largely conservative, orthodox lives, did not step out for anything. Even female roles in the wildly popular Marathi theatre were performed by male actors. Prashant Talwalkar, the present head of Talwalkar's and the grandson of the gym chain's patriarch, Vishnupant, claims, 'This one insight of my grandfather way back in 1943 has defined the trajectory of brand Talwalkar's to this date.' With the entry of females, albeit in 'women-only' hours, Talwalkar's became positioned as a 'family' gym, as opposed to a male 'akhara'.

Today Talwalkar's is the largest chain of fitness centres in India, with over 175 gyms in 65 cities. Prashant Talwalkar—a third generation in the fitness business—is the current chief of the company. From those pioneering days, to today's times, everything about Talwalkar's has transformed, except the core ethos of being a gym for the whole family. While Talwalkar's has always had more men members than women, yet all its strategies are shaped with the acid test of women members' acceptance in mind. All aspects of the gym, its design, equipment, programmes and promotions, and even its trainers, have to pass this test. It's a simple strategy. If it doesn't work for women, it doesn't work for the gym.

Men and women are essentially differently oriented towards a gym. One of Prashant Talwalkar's insights is that men are basic users of the gym. Men's satisfaction is linked to the functional elements of the gym. An uncrowded, hygienic, and modern gym with all the latest equipments in working order is all that men look for. They have a clinical attitude towards their gym. A gym is a place for exercising, period. Women's needs are far different and more complex. To begin with, women look for results. In their pursuit of achieving goals, women look at every aspect of the gym and are more involved with it. They use more features, services, and therefore are also good payers! They use the service aspect of the gym involving care, training, and advice more fully. They are early adopters of various programmes introduced by the gym. For example, it was women who first checked-out Talwalkar's nutrition centres. New initiatives like the weight gain/loss programme found their first takers amongst women. Men too caught on, but more gradually. Prashant describes it thus, 'Women are very demanding on themselves, for weight, shape, beauty; they keep us relevant in their lives and our business flourishing, longer.'

During summer vacations, lady members also influence and bring their kids for short summer programmes at the gyms. 'It's a curious fact that dads never bring children to the gym, moms do!'

The fitness scene in India has completely changed in the past ten years. Players like Talwalkar's are big beneficiaries of lifestyle elements and glamour coming into fitness. Gymming has rapidly moved from being a lifestyle, fashion statement, to a necessity. The organised sector fitness industry in India alone is over $ 600 million in size according to a global trade body. The unorganised sector is also fairly large. The transformation of Bollywood actors—both male and female—on fitness quotient, has been their biggest marketing influencer, a free-of-cost sales force! Like beauty and grooming services, fitness services are the new mainstream professions and businesses are growing rapidly.

Talwalkar's has kept pace with the increasing participation of the upper middle-class Indians in fitness and their rising aspirations. To this end, they enhanced their brand credibility by introducing global-quality modern equipment. The Talwalkar's Academy created a skilled force of trainers that knew the latest fitness techniques and was trained in customer service. The aspiring new customers want them to be so.

Talwalkar's growth can be attributed to its combination of a middle-class environment and a state-of-the-art bouquet of services. They believe that if it's relevant, it must be offered. Therefore they have enhanced their core service of an equipment-driven gym with additional offerings like aerobics and zoomba, trends that are totally international. With such additions, Talwalkar's becomes a neighbourhood gym with an international range of services, an irresistible combination. In keeping with the Indian need for personalised service, the company has created an entire cadre of personal trainers to service individual clients. As with 'tutors' in schools, personal trainers immediately improve results for the clients and revenues for the gyms.

Fitness centres are peculiar in one aspect. They are just about the only business where the customer comes to the 'store' every day. Gyms have to be geared for a more frequent customer contact than any restaurant, beauty salon, or even the neighbourhood grocer! The 12 noon customer expects her trainer to be as fresh and as interested as s/he was to the 6 am customer. It raises a question about staff practices. Talwalkar's understand this and have evolved their own measures and standards to ensure that their trainers are always at their best. One peculiar way they ensure this standard is by having no human resources function. From the leadership family to every gym manager, everyone stays completely hands-on, and meets customers and associates as a part of their daily job. 'We are in the business that involves literal "contact" with the customers. We all need a first-hand feel; there is no place for layers in the people function,' Prashant puts it in context.

Talwalkar's is modernising rapidly with times. People expect newer techniques, faster results. There are functional foods, new assisted-specialist programmes like EMS (electro muscular stimulation), etc. The launch of their first gym in a mall was received with an unprecedented enrolment response. Prashant says, 'There we learnt that ours was the only gym in the market that had 200 car parks in the morning, while the mall stores were yet to open at 11am!'

However, what's most creditable is their shared, strong understanding of what Talwalkar's stands for and especially what it does not. In Prashant Talwalkar's words, 'We have to respond to the market and opportunities, but we cannot go after unproven, non-scientific fads and techniques. People trust us never to do that. Serious fitness is our business; we are not a hangout place.' More importantly, Talwalkar's never do things detached from the Indian ethos and thinking. 'We believe a strong, unstated factor in our favour is that people feel it safe to send their young daughters to Talwalkar's.'

Prashant's clear closing comments are, 'There is nothing wrong with lady personal trainers in gyms wearing hot pants. Our male patrons may like it too. But it does not pass the test of having a congenial, comfortable atmosphere for women patrons. So Talwalkar's will not do it.' Now that's a clear strategy statement! Talwalkar's has proved to be ahead of its time—in recognising women's need for fitness, in reaching out to the middle class and not the rich alone, in remaining grounded and non-faddish, in staying close to the Indian mindset of creating value while following international best practices. Talwalkar's is a completely home-grown business, which has addressed fitness the same way that many other businesses have and succeeded in India, by keeping an ear to the ground and staying close to the customer.

MIND POKE

Are there any upmarket fitness stores/chains in India that unabashedly target male customers only? Are these places doing well?

Tell us on the Supermarketwala Facebook page. Please scan the QR Code using your smartphones to take you directly to the Facebook site.

Beauty Secrets of YLG

SHRUTI KALRA'S DAUGHTER, RHEA, is sixteen years old. Rhea has long, thick black hair, just like her mother, and Shruti devotes her time generously to maintain her daughter's locks. A few days ago, it was time for Rhea's school farewell, and she made known her desire to get her hair styled and coloured. Except that she also wanted to save her hair from the 'damage' that such a transformation would cause. After the party, 'I'll oil my hair at night', Rhea told her mother. It had taken many years of loving care for Rhea's hair to grow to its current glorious state, and neither mother nor daughter was keen on 'ruining' that. Colouring and styling, in most Indian households, is akin to spoiling one's hair. One gets one's hair trimmed to give it shape and bounce, but very few people desire hair that is not long, even if it's shaped well. Everywhere in Indian cities, even the more 'progressive' metros like Mumbai and Bangalore, one sees women who are sporting at least shoulder length hair. Hair, for Indians, is an adornment in itself, a living tissue you nourish, nurture and look after.

Rahul Bhalchandra, a recent entrepreneur and promoter of YLG salons in Bangalore, caught on to this attitude very early in his career. Indians, he discovered, have a strong affinity for long hair. A woman's beauty is incomplete without a swathe of thick, black hair rippling down her back. Long hair plays a key role in most imagery about feminine beauty, for example, in classical poetry and literature. Hair nourishment is central to a woman's beauty regimen and consists chiefly of a regular massage with oil. In fact, most shampoo advertisements portray this ideal of Indian beauty, showing women with thick, swaying hair. Styling is equal to oiling and washing.

Contrast this with what the salon industry is portraying. The biggest service branded salons' offer revolves around hair. The highest paid employees are hair stylists who themselves flaunt hair that looks alien to Indian eyes. Rahul, poetically, compared styled and coloured hair with stilettos. 'Every woman finds them stylish yet uncomfortable, and wants to take them off as soon as they reach home.'

Rahul's main insight about not chasing the western notion of stylised hair is fundamental to the way the salon and the beauty services industry is going to grow in India. In the West, he says, hair colour is variegated. There's brown, black, red, auburn, golden, and many shades in between. People are comfortable with hair being coloured differently for different people. In India, most people, barring a handful of exceptions, have black hair. Thus, in the West, when people wish to look different, they place changing hair colour under active consideration, just as they change the colour of their nail varnish. One might have dark hair one day, and change it to blond the next, merely to look different. In contrast, for Indians, colouring, still, is merely a medium for covering grey. At the most, younger Indians experiment with streaks and highlights, but mostly, even that means stepping out on a limb where beauty is concerned. For most Indians, coloured and treated hair is equated with damaged hair. Hair styling and colouring is, therefore, an occasional indulgence, not essential to one's appearance.

Paradoxically, the biggest offering in salons in India has to do with hair, even though that is what Indians need the least. Rahul has decided to change this paradigm. While in the West, hair has a distinctive identity, in India it is skin. A glowing complexion is considered integral to real beauty. There is differentiation in skin tones, and beauty products for skin are matched to the individual's complexion. At the same time, where professional skin care services are concerned, Rahul has much more leeway. Compared to hair styling, skin care is much more simple to handle, and requires far less training, thus, reducing training and retention overheads for the business.

YLG has identified skincare as a game changer in the beauty business. Even today, the ratio of spend on skin versus hair is 60:40, with only 10 percent of the revenue coming from styling. In salon imagery, of course, the opposite is true. All of us have seen gigantic posters of exquisitely styled hair in salons, most of these sponsored by L'Oreal, the industry leader by far. Skin, with a larger share of the consumer's pocket, is, ironically, mostly under-pitched by the beauty salons industry, even though the customers are clearly indicating with their wallets where their preference lies. The only brand that is trying to make a difference is Kaya. From the house of Marico, Kaya Salons are devoted almost exclusively to sophisticated and high-end skin care.

In a short space of five years, YLG, with 34 salons, 23 of them in Bangalore, has become the market leader, with a 40 percent market share, overtaking the giant, Lakme in Bangalore. How has this come about? It has happened because Bhalchandra understands what the Indian customer is all about. Having identified skincare as its primary business, thus offering more customization and differentiation in this area rather than in hair care, YLG also modified their pricing to reflect the Indian consumer's penchant for value for money, the 'more at any cost' mentality. While Shruti's desire for styling and colouring is sporadic at best, she is very pleased with the YLG loyalty card that allows her to pay an annual fee for a package of services that are 30 percent more expensive if taken individually. There are many loyalty cards that work on this principle. YLG is different because it allows anyone with access to a particular loyalty card to use it. Shruti's card is used very frequently by Rhea. At sixteen, Rhea is a prime candidate for body-hair waxing and visits the salon regularly. In her mind, the service is paid for already, and when there is no cash transaction each time the service is used, it becomes all the more attractive. Bhalchandra knows it's only a matter of time before Rhea starts demanding facial and massage services. Very soon, Shruti's loyalty card will have to be loaded before the year is out, adding to YLG's revenue, and another customer, Rhea, would have got added to their rolls. Both Shruti and Rhea will now visit only YLG, where the huge array of skincare services, including various waxing and massage options, makes it doubly attractive. Revenue, footfalls, and customer loyalty—isn't that what every business is looking for?

YLG is a homegrown business, whose success is based almost entirely on the promoter's insights into what the Indian customer is looking for. The conscious shift away from a multinational's position has paid Bhalchandra rich dividends. While giving the customer exactly what she wants!

Rahul's YLG also dabbles in a new concept—YLG-on-wheels, to try and tap older women and those in more conservative localities. 'Women from the family and sometimes even their neighbours come along for our services once we land up at a customer's home. One needs to stay close to the real world of Indian women, to serve the full market potential and to make salon going a regular habit for women. Else, going to a beautician will remain a marriage and party occasion trip for a large number of women. I like to believe we are changing that,' says Rahul.

YLG, the brand, and its well-discovered take on Indian women's salon needs is now backed by two leading private equity funds. Sure enough, it seems to make sense to go after the large, middle of the market India, and not just its westernised thin layer. We'll be keenly observing this space of the unique YLG Touch! How about you?!

MIND POKE

Like the skincare focus of brands Kaya or YLG, have you come across beauty salon chains or stores that differentiate themselves clearly, in a crowded market? Share examples with us.

Tell us on the Supermarketwala Facebook page. Please scan the QR Code using your smartphones to take you directly to the Facebook site.

The Future Is Here

LOOKING INTO THE FUTURE is an exciting pastime at the best of times. To gaze into the unknown, and study the present to predict the future is something that no human being can resist indulging in. If we discount astrology, then we can categorically state that science is all about predicting the future by calculating present events. But what if the future is already here? What if things are changing in front of our very eyes at a speed that's hard to comprehend rationally? What if something happens almost before one can predict it? The outcome can be both exciting and frightening. For the student, change offers huge possibilities and heady challenges. For the status quoist, change is merely another headache, to be borne, rather than celebrated. It doesn't need stating that success belongs to those who embrace change.

The story of modern retail in India is a story based in the future, and that future is here. Let us look at the 'future' consumer in this story. Has modern retail changed her? Can anything as commonplace as the act of buying a shampoo 'reframe' a human being? The answer is yes. In the past, the customer was a passive being, one who went to the store, requested the man behind the counter to give her a set of items and returned, almost unchanged by the transaction. If there was anything that had an influence on the customer, it was advertising and its communication of the attributes of the product. Today, modern retail has changed that entire framework, almost turned it on its head. In a self-service store, the customer starts consuming even before she enters the store. Take a supermarket. At the entrance, there are a stack of baskets and a row of trolleys. This is decision time, right here! The act of choosing has already begun. A shopping cart indicates higher involvement, and consequently, more alert senses. In a traditional store, the faculty the customer uses the most is her speech. She has to ask for things. Not much else is involved in the transaction. In modern retail, on the other hand, she touches the product, looks at the aisles, hears the offers that are constantly being announced over the PA system, gets a taste of new brands of beverages or biscuits or waffles, smells the new deo and applies some sample body lotion on her skin. Garments on hangars are evaluated for colour, cut, design and then tried on before selection. Every single sense is involved, including her brain that is actively engaging with the environment. She is constantly doing the math. What is the promise of one product versus the other? How much discount does this store offer compared to another one? Is it better to buy a larger pack size now, or two smaller ones in the future? Is it worth paying the premium on a new launch, or wait for a few months for prices to drop? Choice, choice, and more choice—the customer is surrounded by it. She is at the centre of everything, and her sense of empowerment is immense. Self-service shopping irreversibly impacts the customer's self-image. No longer is she dependent on another's judgment or greater proximity to the goods. She is no longer subservient to another person when it comes to consuming. The power belongs to her, and more significantly, she knows it.

Now the picture is clear. Whether it is a cake of soap or one's wedding outfit, self-service, the cornerstone of modern retail, heightens the customer's sense of power, and having tasted this empowerment once, she finds it difficult to go back to the shopkeeper-driven format. Self-service shopping, as social commentator Santosh Desai says, 'Makes consumption a lot more tactile. You "consume" the product in various ways, see it, pick it, feel it, smell it at the shelf and even wear it before buying, paying for, owning and therefore actually consuming it. In economist's terms the consumer surplus kicks in much before the commercial act of buying. Indeed, the very fact that they shop in a mall improves the self-image of people.'

Modern retail delivers a significantly more involved and interested consumer to the brands, in a positive environment of abundant choice. This willing and eager mindset also makes this consumer more willing to switch brands and try your competitor. Marketers who're living in this future are adapting their brands' energies to this reality. Once self-service is introduced, there's no going back. The power of choosing has shifted to the consumer and traditional forms of advertising, selling, even pricing, have to fall in line with this reality. Marketers who wait for modern retail to be volume significant in India to move their mindset, are playing with risky myopia in my opinion. Another peculiar thing about retail in India is, most of its leadership is from the branded consumer products pedigree. These retailers have been through the same consumer centric training that the brand marketers have been through. They know a consumer behaviour shift when they see one.

Products and brands need to tune into this new context—of the asserting consumer and the new theatre of choice that put her in the centre. If marketers do not 'think' their brand in this new shopping syntax, their learning curve and learning cost will be steeper. India will be one of the largest consumer markets within a decade. The prize of success here is huge. It will be silly to not tune in to its nuances. Most consumer goods categories are, in fact, waiting to be discovered. The big consumption wave is still ahead of us. Paradoxically, while the customer is ready for the future, most marketers and retailers are still fumbling in their ways. Whenever they've got their act together, their success has been startling.

An even bigger wave

But wait—not so fast! Just as the customer has become 'sensorially enhanced' and has begun challenging marketers used to traditional retail, another and even larger change is building up. And the name of that change is—DIGITAL. In fact, my prediction is that the digital shopping revolution is going to skip over the self-service, physical shopping stage. This isn't the star-gazing variety of prediction, but based on empirical evidence. We have the very solid example of mobile telephony in front of us. India's telecom revolution skipped the stage of landline connectivity to go straight to mobile telephony. The lack of infrastructure forced a rethink on approaching the customer. Almost the same situation exists in retail. While physical infrastructure in terms of urban spaces and facilities is growing at a leisurely pace, the Internet facilitation is happening even as we speak. While we talk of a digital revolution, the real revolution in digital technology is going to happen with the launch of the 4G data network, when information exchange will happen as close to real time as possible. In transaction terms this means that we will consume at home at the same speed as we do in physical spaces, be it media content or shopping, but even more interactively. The possibilities this situation throws up are mind-boggling, and we can almost play a game of extending our imagination as marketers and retailers to the hilt. A paradigm shift is hurtling towards us at supersonic speed, and not many of us are even partially ready for it.

The machine age was all about increasingly overcoming the limitations of the body—of effort, fatigue, travel etc. The digital age is about overcoming the limitations of the mind. 'If you can imagine it, it can happen, seems to be its poetic promise,' is Santosh Desai's interpretation. 'For instance, earlier, you tried a frock on and if you were to imagine it in different colours, you would shut your eyes and imagine. Now you'll open your eyes in the trial room, touch a colour of choice and see,' he chuckles. It is hard to imagine the collapse of thought and action, but it has already started happening. In a few years from now, this will be mainstream, hard as it is to believe today. For customers sitting in distant parts of the country, the absence of infrastructure is no longer a barrier to consuming more. The Internet plugs the gap fairly well. Flipkart and Jabong attract Mrs Patnaik in distant Raigada extremely effectively, and the absence of changing rooms and mirrors is only a minor hindrance to consumption.

Think the Internet, think the elite. Or so one believes of India. In fact, it's the other way around. Just as the humblest carpenter is now completely dependent on his mobile phone for business, so will the Internet become an enabler for reaching consumption to the least literate consumer. This sounds counter-intuitive but actually isn't. With the new language of the digital world—watch, touch, swipe, drag, drop – there is no literacy or knowledge barrier to doing things digital. We've all seen toddlers and even grandparents enjoying their new freedom with the picture, video and touch screens. No longer does a three year old have to wait for her parent to turn on the TV button. The iPad has become the ultimate media behemoth. Web shopping? Just watch this small video on YouTube—look for 'La Rebaja Movil'. This two and a half minute video is my bet for how grandma will shop for groceries in the next wave.

As for access, as we saw in the chapter on 'Chedda Internet Supermarket', the enterprising bunch of micro-retailers in India will bridge the digital access and literacy gap in ways that are unique. By accessing the power of e commerce and its infinite range availability, the neighbourhood small stores will also be able to meet all our needs. I would hazard a guess that in year 2020, a Bengali customer living in distant Coimbatore, will be able to get her fresh palm jaggery (nolen gur) during winter, ordered for her from Kolkata by her corner grocery store in Coimbatore! All niches can be served in the new age.

How do we get ready for this digital shopping wave if we are a hypermarket? A mass brand? A niche brand? Or a regional brand? The lessons are different for each one of us but rapid learning and adapting is something we'll all need to do.

To keep up with the secrets to winning consumer India, I'll be watching the progress of the self–service wave and the arrival of the true digital shopping wave, very carefully. I hope most of us learn to ride these waves and benefit from them while making fewer mistakes.

Lets continue engaging our imagination at Supermarketwala Facebook page or @Supermarketwala on twitter. Until then…

Acknowledgements

I WAS NOT MEANT to write. I run shops, sell things in my day job and chat with curious people in my spare time. But for Indrajit Gupta 'IG', who was till recently Editor at Forbes India, I would not be writing at all. IG told me that while everyone spoke of space, capital, and supply chain, I spoke the consumer's language in retail, and I should share my thoughts. Many business and trade publications provided me a platform for writing. Forbes India gave me an invitation blog and that is where Milee Aishwarya of Random House found me and decided my thoughts were worthy of a book. Thanks to all these people, you are reading *Supermarketwala*.

In a society where it is normal to be in a follower mind-set and to look up to western markets for all that stands for progress and wisdom, I have been lucky to have walked alongside two amazing original thinkers and business builders. Radhakishan Damani and Kishore Biyani, while learning from everyone, never cared much for validation of their thoughts from anyone or anywhere, except the Indian consumers at their stores. Many hours of working in the stores with them, trying new tricks with the customers, making mistakes together, have made me the retailer I am today.

Kishore Biyani surrounded himself with fearless

consumer champions and I especially benefitted from my exchanges with Rajan Malhotra, Anand Adukia, Raj Banerjee, Venkateshwar Kumar, Sanjeev Agrawal and Sadashiv Nayak from the Big Bazaar team. Dear colleagues Arvind Choudhary, Narendra Baheti and his brothers Rajendra and Govind, gave me a window into the Indian trading communities and their ways of working. My insight digging habit was ably supported by a young set of innovators—Ashni Biyani, Omendu Prakash, Preeti Vyas, Rishabh Arora, Mustafa Merchant, Dali Agarwal, Hemang Savla, and Mayank Tandon—who led me to every possible place where people exchanged goods and conversation, across a 'continent' called India. Our trip to the oldest marketplace city of Banaras, with Bhagi Jalan was a high point of our journeys. Shruti Gandhi and Kurush Pavri chased many tentative new ideas as projects for me. With this team of youngsters, everything was possible. We even wrote the script for a Bollywood movie, set in a hypermarket!

The teams at FutureBrands under Santosh Desai, especially Atulit Saxena and Anand Pandey, and at Idiom Design, led by Jacob, Sonia, and Girish, were part of dozens of imagination and brand creation sessions over the years. I always envied them for having 'decoding insights and imagining'—something I did as a business hobby—was their day job! Ireena Vittal from Mckinsey also added crucial facets to my thinking, during my writings.

Hindustan Unilever shaped my professional worldview. I learnt to call my consumer 'she' at Levers. Keki Dadiseth made a crucial difference to my then tangential thinking on the retail opportunity. Nitin Paranjpe and Shrijeet Mishra have been friends I have depended on, for their professional inputs and personal support at all times. HUL has given me a whole bunch of bright friends and guides who I can reach out to, anywhere in the world.

In Reliance Retail, I have gained further ground in the science of retail and combined it with thinking large scale. Manojbhai Modi provides bold challenges and provokes a push for the next level ambition, continuously. Rob Cissel and Shawn Gray from Wal-mart, Shivram Murti, Madhvan, Ram Somatia, and Pankaj Pawar have added to my perspective. Sanjay Jog, an old ally and trusted friend, always points me in the right direction.

Many stories and lessons in this book have been researched and crafted with two consumer research specialists and dear friends Piyul Mukherjee and Deepa Soman. Indeed, Piyul and I together wrote my first published piece in the *Times of India*. Deepa's all-women team at Lumiere Business Solutions has been my go-to place for research and insight validation. Lumiere specifically worked with me on the 'winning brands' section of the book. In recent years, two amazing sociologists became my avid conversation partners. The first, Tejaswini Adhikari of TISS started as an irate customer at my store and the other, Dnyanada Deshpande did an interview with me on a television channel! They always provide the missing societal link in my interpretations. Many observations of mine have been churned, dissected, garnished, celebrated, and even trashed in the company of these four very bright thought partners.

Prof. Piyush Sinha from the Centre for Retailing at IIM Ahmedabad and Dr Uday Salunke and his dynamic team at WeSchool Mumbai, gave me the valuable opportunity for academic and student engagement. I am grateful for their continuous encouragement. I never studied retail in college. My first formal teacher, when I launched my stores was Misraji—Shri S. C. Misra. I am grateful to him for teaching me to read meaning into point-of-sale data and showing me dozens of norms applicable to Indian supermarkets. Misraji, along with Chetan Sangoi is an authority on running independent self-service stores. In my early retail days, Natwar Mall, Rama Tadepalli, Savitri Dadhich were people who shaped and encouraged my thought, as willing sounding boards.

Milee Aishwarya of Random House publishers made it sound so easy, when we started off on this book. Many missed deadlines and persuasions later the team of Milee Aishwarya and Debdatta Das have had me complete their book project. Penguin Random House design team have brilliantly designed the cover and my talented artist and design friend Omendu Prakash added just the crucial zing to it. Omendu has also done all the illustrations for the book, in his original style.

Now, to some home truths. My wife Sangeeta, a twice published novelist, has done her Masters in Creative Writing. She is the 'intel inside' of writing in this book. Many a chapters have got argued and hammered into shape during our endless walks together. Without her vital inputs this work would have taken three more years to be in your hands. Harsh and Yash, our ever so talented Doon boys, also pitched in with little tips from stores they went to. They both are also the musical influence around me. Sangeeta comes from a family of intellectuals. People often say, how come in a family of writers, teachers and music lovers, I am this 'born to be a grocer', shopkeeper?! It happens...

A Note on the Author

When Damodar Mall got his first job as a management trainee at Hindustan Unilever Limited, traditionalists around him were shocked by his choice of employment. How could a graduate of IIT, Mumbai and IIM, Bangalore, work as a seller of soap and oil, they asked! Damodar did one better, he moved on to become a seller of rice and daal, a profession that till then was restricted only to the trader community all across the country!

Since his first venture that was subsequently built into the super-successful DMart chain, Damodar has been at the helm for two major players in the modern retail industry, Big Bazaar and now, Reliance Value Retail. His love affair with organised retail is going strong even after fifteen years, and his mission is to get at least one fresh consumer insight from his environment every day.

When he's not being a grocer, Damodar loves to play the keyboard, a passion that he acquired from his two musician sons. Damodar lives with his wife Sangeeta, a published novelist, in Mumbai. *Supermarketwala* is his first book.